An Executive's Guide to

Reverse Logistics

How to Find Hidden Profits by Managing Returns

by CURTIS GREVE
and JERRY DAVIS

ISBN: 0983551405
ISBN 13: 9780983551409

Contents

Curtis Greve's Dedication

This book is dedicated to my mother Anna Greve.
You are dearly missed.

<'(((><

Jerry Davis' Dedication

I dedicate this book to my wife Sandy.

Foreward

by Dr. Dale S. Rogers

I first met Curtis Greve and Jerry Davis in the mid-1990s. They were working for a company that was developing the idea of reverse logistics and returns management for several major retailers. Curtis had just left Walmart as the head of reverse logistics and returns. He had many ideas as to how reverse logistics could actually grow into a discipline that would be taught in universities, and become a respected career path for many managers. Jerry was the COO of a company providing reverse logistics and together they both worked to develop reverse logistics solutions that would be adopted across the globe.

The book you are about to read is an excellent overview of the state-of-the-art in reverse logistics. Curtis and Jerry have done a good job of thinking through exactly how reverse logistics and returns management can impact a company. They explain clearly how reverse logistics impacts a firm's customers, suppliers, partners, service providers, and shareholder value. There is a clear message about sustainability included in this book as well. They highlight the importance of many different activities that are key parts of the reverse logistics process and how those activities impact the supply chain and a company's bottom line.

What once was an afterthought in most corporations has become a respected and important part of a corporation's infrastructure.

This book also explains how to develop reverse logistics programs when scarce resources are often applied to other needs of the corporation. One of the biggest problems with innovating a returns management program within an organization is that an organization has many demands on its scarce resources, and reverse logistics is quite often not perceived to be one of the most pressing needs. This book will explain how you make a case for implementing reverse logistics, and how they can actually drive profit to your company's bottom line.

I think this book will be quite useful both for executives as the title implies, but also for researchers and students that would like to understand what is common practice and best practices in reverse logistics and returns management in North America. Based on their extensive experience the authors have put a great deal of thought into difficult issues that are typical in a corporation.

Reverse logistics has many faces. It can be consumer returns, marketing returns asset returns, damage returns, return avoidance, gatekeeping and many other types of issues. It is clear that good reverse logistics management helps keep customers happy by reducing their risk and ensuring the corporation will continue to have a long-term relationship with its consumers. The authors write that Walmart used reverse logistics to keep customers happy, one return at a time. That message still resonates at Walmart and the other successful retailers today.

Over the years Curtis and Jerry have become great friends of mine. We have spent hundreds of hours thinking about reverse logistics and many other issues. They have traveled around the world with me talking to companies and organizations about how to best manage returns. It has been really fun to hang out with them, learn from them, and share their lives. They are good people and I think they have written a good book. I am sure you will both enjoy it, and learn something.

Dr. Dale S. Rogers
Professor, Logistics & Supply Chain Management
Co-Director, Center for Supply Chain Management
Rutgers University

About the Authors

"I have found in the course of our joint services that I think right when I think with you."

— Thomas Jefferson to John Adams

Curtis Greve and Jerry Davis, the principals of Greve-Davis, were pioneers in the field of reverse logistics and today are recognized thought leaders in their industry. Curtis and Jerry have been working in the field of reverse logistics since the birth of the industry in the 1980's. Together they have over 60 years of experience in reverse logistics and supply chain management.

Greve-Davis offers clients the benefit of their real-world, reverse logistics experience. They are innovators in return center development and operations; third-party, vendor, and union contract negotiation; liquidation rate improvement; and software selection, design and installation. Depth and breath of knowledge with over 60 years of experience in reverse supply chain management; this is why Greve-Davis is widely considered the premiere reverse logistics consulting firm in the world.

The History of Greve-Davis

In 2008, Curtis Greve started his own consulting firm with a vision of providing solutions that would add significant value to companies by improving their reverse logistics capabilities and maximizing the value of assets in the reverse logistics channel. In 2010, Jerry Davis joined Curtis to form Greve-Davis – The Reverse Logistics Experts.

Together, Jerry and Curtis have over 60 years experience in reverse logistics, third party logistics management, contract negotiations, returns operations management, and product liquidation.

Greve-Davis works with clients to increase profits by improving return center operations, increase liquidation recovery rates, improve returns policy management, and maximize the benefits of outsourcing. Clients include third party service providers, liquidators, retailer, manufacturers, and distributors. All have unique issues with returns and significant opportunities to improve their bottom line by improving their reverse logistics capabilities.

Curtis Greve

Prior to starting Greve-Davis, Curtis Greve spent 15 years at Genco, a leading third party logistics company (3PL), and prior to that worked for Wal-Mart Stores for 12 years. Throughout his time at Genco, Curtis was a member of the senior staff, during which time he was directly responsible for all reverse logistics customers, operations and systems; including pharmaceutical returns and damage research businesses. Curtis was responsible for HR, IT, and retail distribution center operations over the course of his career at Genco as well. He was a key senior executive that helped lead Genco from being a small regional 3PL to North America's second largest warehouse based 3PL.

In addition to his responsibilities over three business units and various corporate departments, Curtis lead the effort to expand Genco's business into Europe. As part of this, Curtis studied the 3PL market extensively and eventually negotiated a joint venture agreement with Wincanton, a leading European 3PL. Curtis also represented Genco on the board of their Indian joint venture. Initially responsible for operations, having ran the world's largest return center at Wal-Mart for four years, Curtis also found success selling Genco services. His ability to sell and his position lead to being assigned responsibility over all sales and marketing functions, in addition to his other responsibilities.

While Curtis wore many hats at Genco, he had a wide variety of experiences at Wal-Mart as well. Curtis worked for Wal-Mart for

12 years where he held number of positions including Corporate Audit Manager, Wal-Mart Supercenter Controller, and Vice President of Reverse Logistics. He worked on the team that initially designed Sam's Club back office processes, lead the re-engineering efforts on Wal-Mart stores invoice office functions, developed the Construction Audit process and rewrote the Wal-Mart's Store Audit program.

Along with these achievements, while heading up returns management and reverse logistics at Wal-Mart, Curtis designed the network of facilities that is used today to efficiently process returns from across the US. He was the driving forces behind the development of operational KPI's, the first incentive program for hourly worker in the returns center, designed and oversaw installation of the first reverse logistics system application, and developed many back office processes and functions that enabled Wal-Mart to realize a **285.0% decrease** in reverse logistics costs over his four year tenure. Perhaps Curtis' proudest achievement was when his Bentonville Return Center, with over 375 employees, set a safety record for Wal-Mart's Distribution Facilities by going over two years without a lost time accident.

Jerry Davis

Jerry Davis is a reverse logistics and supply chain expert with over forty years of experience in a variety of industries and disciplines. Today, Mr. Davis is a recognized thought leader in reverse logistics and supply chain management. Jerry is also known as a skilled negotiator and executive coach.

Jerry's skills and capabilities are best expressed by the CEO of Mancini's Bakery who said "On the labor front he (Jerry Davis) steered the course of our negotiations from abashed confrontation to professional and amiable sessions. He did this with respect integrity and firmness. His leadership skills and management expertise enabled him to present my company with five very favorable outcomes." The CEO went on to say "Mr. Davis has made recommendations that have seen me through family business difficulties, outrageous commodity pricing, trademark problems, delicate employee situations, and customer acquisition and retention issues."

Jerry began his career after service in the U.S. Army, including two tours in Vietnam during which he received the Bronze Star with an Oak Leaf Cluster. After serving his country, Jerry attended the University of South Carolina where he studied business.

A life-long resident of Western Pennsylvania, Mr. Davis advanced quickly throughout his "first career" in the supermarket industry. From a humble receiving clerk to the president of the OK Grocery Company, the wholesale division of Giant Eagle Markets (one of the nation's leading supermarket companies), Mr. Davis developed logistics skills and expertise that enabled him to successfully lead 2,000 employees in building a company with sales in excess of one billion dollars. During his tenure, Mr. Davis was responsible for all distribution, transportation, buying, acquisitions, start-ups and labor relations functions of the corporation. Mr. Davis became nationally recognized in the forward logistics industry. He served as the chairman of the Food Marketing Institute's Distribution Committee and testified before Congress multiple times on behalf of the food industry. He also was a founding director of the Greater Pittsburgh Community Food Bank and served on the Board of Directors of the Pittsburgh Chapter of the American Red Cross, Junior Achievement, The Holy Family Institute and several committee positions for the United Way. He was named as a Citizen Ambassador to the Soviet Union by the U.S. State Department.

Years of real-world experience and success positioned him as uniquely qualified to begin his "second career" in 1990 when Mr. Davis founded Scanning Solutions. He recognized that the forward logistics industry was only half of the equation for retailers and manufacturers needing to close the logistics loop by effectively processing or recycling consumer returns and un-saleable. While some companies were beginning to recognize the need for an efficient way to handle returns in the early 1990s, it was Mr. Davis who had the vision to develop a sophisticated software solution and couple it with a solid, third-party logistics operation; making his company the pioneer in the reverse logistics industry. Following Scanning Solutions' merger with Genco, at that time a small public warehouse company in Pittsburgh, PA, Mr. Davis became vice chairman of that company where he was responsible for its development into a world-class provider of reverse logistics services. Under his leadership, the company grew to over six million square feet of warehouse space, achieved over $600,000,000 in sales and had 4,000 employees. His customers were a who's who list of major retailers and manufacturers in North America.

Introduction

Reverse logistics, or returns management, is an often-overlooked link in an organization's supply chain. For the majority of supply chain executives, the returns function is the most disorganized, least attended to aspect of warehouse operations. The returns department overflows with damaged or outdated product that executives do not like to walk by, much less do anything about. It is difficult for the average supply chain executive to get excited about reverse logistics because returns are not pretty and their impact on the company is not clearly understood. Further, most supply chain executives are not measured or paid based on how well they perform in the reverse logistics arena. Effective returns management is a subject that is easy to dismiss. Let's face it. Overcoming "ugly and confusing", without a clear financial incentive to do so, is incredibly difficult.

However, according to a February 2010 study by The Aberdeen Group, companies categorized as best-in-class in returns processing averaged a ninety-three percent customer satisfaction rating. This customer satisfaction rating is twelve percent higher than the eighty percent of companies surveyed that are not considered best-in-class. (1) The lesson is clear. Focusing on returns processing and reverse logistics, pays off in better customer satisfaction.

Most executives are surprised at the dollar value of the assets that flow through the reverse logistics pipeline in the United States. According to a white paper written by Dr. James Stock of the University of South Florida, U.S. consumers annually return product with a dollar value that is greater than the GDP of sixty-six percent of the nations in the world. (2) In addition to the enormous volume of consumer returns, four hundred and ninety-five mandatory product recalls were issued by the Consumer Protection Agency, two hundred and ninety-five pharmaceutical recalls were issued by the Food and Drug Administration (FDA) and an estimated eight hundred voluntary manufacturers' recalls were initiated in 2009 alone. (3)

As we will discuss later, much of this merchandise is destroyed, some is refurbished or remanufactured, some is held for reintroduction next season, and about half is sold on the secondary retail market. According to a study conducted by Dr. Dale S. Rogers, professor in The Department of Supply Chain Management and Marketing Sciences at Rutgers University and formerly, Director of the Center for Logistics Management at the University of Nevada at Reno, the secondary market equates to $329 billion or 2.28% of U.S. Gross Domestic Product (GDP). (4 page 136) Clearly reverse logistics is big money and has a big impact on every company that is involved in producing, distributing, or selling goods.

The National Retail Federation (NRF) reported that the rate of return of consumer goods sold in 2009 was over eight percent of total sales. (5) The same survey reported that fifty-eight percent of retailers used a manual system to track and account for returns. (page 5) These are shocking statistics! Over half of U.S. retailers lost track of billions of dollars of returned goods by not utilizing available technology and processes. As a result,, during 2009 the average retailer in the U.S. tracked of over 8% of their inventory manually and had limited visibility of what was actually returned or exactly what happened to it.

For manufacturers, the picture isn't any better. A 2006 Aberdeen Group study reported that the cost of processing returns for hard goods manufacturers ranges from nine percent to 14.6 percent of sales. (6) Just like their retail counterparts, over sixty percent of manufacturers did not track what was returned. Further, the manufacturers surveyed called out the need for a tracking system that would provide the needed visibility. (page 11)

When surveyed by the Aberdeen Group in 2010 both retailers and manufacturers rated returns management as "very important". (page 17) Yet, the majority of these companies, because of an admitted lack of visibility and processing capabilities are virtually blind to assets in their reverse logistics pipeline. This blindness makes it difficult to positively impact the negative cost of returns management.

Look at the implications of these two studies from a "reverse point of view." Return rates average eight percent of retail sales, cost manufacturers from nine to 14.6 percent of sales to process, and impact customer satisfaction by as much as twelve percent, yet are virtually ignored by the majority of executive management worldwide.

One might wonder why? Why would top business leaders, universally admired captains of industry, ignore a function that could improve customer satisfaction by twelve percent or more? Why would companies known for their controls and discipline allow eight percent of their inventory to fall into a black hole with little or no tracking, controls or visibility? Why would corporations known for their ability to focus their team and execute strategy ignore a process that costs from nine to 14.6 percent of sales?

The answer is perspective and resources. Perspective can be elusive because few look at returns as requiring a process. Only the most visionary consider reverse logistics as a pipeline or even a reverse supply chain. A CEO may see that their return rate is up from eight to ten percent after Christmas, but few have visibility to the total cost of processing those returns. Few organizations track basic metrics that show the true net cost of returns to the company. While every executive understands the importance of customer communications, few look at their return policies and associated procedures to see if they are causing customer dissatisfaction or creating trouble with their business partners up and down the supply chain. In late 2010, in response to customer complaints, Best Buy relaxed its policy on restocking fees. (7) However, more than eighty-three percent of companies have not changed their returns policies. (7) Will Best Buy garner an even larger share of the consumer electronics business as a result of the act of listening to their customers?

Often, when companies do take a look at the reverse pipeline, they are reluctant to commit resources, manpower, or money to improve the process. This is true from the boardroom to the warehouse floor. Vice presidents of manufacturing and supply chain executives worldwide typically don't get fired because they do a bad job processing returned product. Their bonuses may be dependent on many goals and many metrics but seldom do they have anything to do with returns processing. Even if they did focus their talent and resources on returns, most companies don't know where or how to begin, nor do they have the experience needed to address the issues with improvements that will put money on the bottom line.

For most companies, the result is that reverse logistics is ignored and neglected. Unfortunately, this trend will continue until executives discover the hidden profits in managing returns and become committed to maximizing the bottom line of their company and improving customer relations.

Reverse logistics is an opportunity to develop a competitive advantage that could result in increasing profits by five percent or more. (8) That's right. For many companies, they have the opportunity to increase net earnings as much as five percent simply by focusing on improving their reverse logistics capabilities.

It is precisely because of the significant financial opportunities and lack of reverse logistics knowledge and experience that this book has been written.

This book will cover the basic issues encountered in reverse logistics management. It is aimed at executives who suddenly find themselves responsible for their company's returns process or executives that want to become a hero by making dramatic improvements in customer satisfaction and profits. It will share over forty years of best practices in reverse logistics that the reader can use to improve their reverse processes and maximize the value of the assets processed.

This book will discuss how to structure return policies and supplier agreements. We will examine return center operations and best practices, returns systems development, and liquidation of product on the secondary market. The best practices outlined in this book are applicable to manufacturers, retailers, e-tailers, as well as distributors. Anyone involved in the forward supply chain will find this book enlightening and useful. Sustainability executives will find this book very helpful because we will examine the many ways sustainability efforts will become financially viable when coupled with a quality reverse logistics solution.

The fact is every aspect of any company who manufactures, ships, or sells goods to a customer is impacted to some degree by reverse logistics. Likewise, a company's reverse logistics processes impact virtually every constituency of a company including internal support functions; sales, operations; suppliers; and most importantly, customers.

Our hope is that this book will shine the light of understanding into the dark recesses of the reverse supply chain to maximize the value of returned assets, develop more sustainable practices, improve customer service, and ultimately enable you to make more money for your company.

Those of us who are blessed with success owe many people who shaped our lives and careers. I would like to thank my mother and my sister. They raised me during a time when widows did not get a lot of help or support. They taught me the value of a good day's work and the importance of family. If there is anything that is good in me, it is because of them.

I would also like to thank Lee Scott. He took a chance by promoting me and literally forcing me to assume responsibility for the return center at Walmart. For four years, I had the opportunity to meet with him every other week for a one-on-one training session. He taught me how to treat people. By his example, I learned how real leaders conduct themselves.

Finally, I would like to thank my partner and mentor Jerry Davis. My father died when I was two years old. I would like to think he and Jerry would have a lot in common. Jerry taught me how to run a business, how to lead people, how to deal with controversy, how to treat my family. I value his guidance and friendship beyond measure. I was lucky to work for him for over ten years and I'm blessed to have him as my partner today.

My hope is that you will find some valuable information in this book that will help improve your reverse logistics program and improve your company's bottom line.

Curtis Greve

CHAPTER 1

What is Reverse Logistics?

Reverse Logistics has been defined as the process of moving goods from their typical final destination for the purpose of capturing value or for proper disposal. (9) Another way of saying this is reverse logistics is the removal of assets from their primary channel of use to a secondary channel in a manner that maximizes the value of those assets. Reverse logistics incorporates returns management; aftermarket services; field services; refurbishing goods; repair activities; recycling; liquidation; related policies and agreements; as well as recall activities, repackaging, and general repurposing of assets.

Any business that sells product of any kind, to any type of customer has to deal with returns; damage; and in some cases, recalls. The processes surrounding the receipt and processing of these transactions all come under the heading of reverse logistics. Throughout this book, the terms reverse logistics and returns management will be used interchangeably. These outlined theories, definitions, and best practices will apply equally to retailers, manufacturers, service providers and distributors.

The Impact of Reverse Logistics

Regardless of the category a business falls into, reverse logistics impacts customers, suppliers, partners, service providers, the environment, corporate earnings, and shareholder value. A company's ability to effectively interact with their customers during the "return experience"; process recalled and returned assets; deal fairly and accurately with all trading partners; financially account for the returns process; and manage the ultimate disposition of the asset in a responsible manner will positively impact customer satisfaction, business reputation, sales, earnings, public opinion, and shareholder value.

Executive's Reaction to Reverse Logistics

Executives typically react in one of two ways when reverse logistics discussions are initiated. The first, and most common, reaction is to oversimplify reverse logistics as nothing more than "returns". The customer brings stuff back, they get money, they buy more stuff, we write off the junk. For those with this mind-set, there is generally a huge opportunity to put enormous amounts of money on the bottom line. However, motivation to take action and commit resources can be a problem due to the lack of understanding and myopic view of returns processing and the reverse logistics pipeline.

The second type of executive reaction you tend to get of reverse logistics issues is one of hopeless acceptance. "It is what it is." "It is very complicated". Reverse logistics crosses departmental boundaries. There are few or no internal resources available to focus on reverse logistics. No single executive is generally responsible for reverse logistics and, usually, no one volunteers to take it on. Returns are ugly. Reverse logistics often flies under the radar. Supply chain executives view returns as an enormous, unwanted problem with little or no benefit to their priority, forward-logistics responsibilities. Merchants don't like to talk about returns, and operations executives just want it out of their way.

Executives who fall into the "returns are hopeless" category are actually closer to a big payoff than those who simply see "returns" as "returns". "Hopeless" executives at least understand it is more complicated and far-reaching than simply returned goods. It is for these reasons that it typically takes a chief financial officer (CFO) to champion the corporate reverse logistics effort. Finding an internal champion is the first, most important, step to finding the hidden profits in a company's languishing returns. But before examining this fact, there are some basic understandings that need to be established.

Return Centers

For the uninitiated, and at first glance, a return center facility looks like a much smaller, easier process than a big distribution facility with its miles of conveyor, multi-level pick modules, and complex warehouse management systems. On many levels this is true. However, do not be deceived. Return center operations are smaller but they are very complex. Like Temple Grandin, noted autistic author and speaker, said: "different, not less." They usually have little or limited material handling equipment, but the variations in terms of handling and processing are much greater than a distribution facility.

The Difference Between Return and Distribution Centers

To help understand the differences between return center operations and a distribution center operations, let us review a few basic processes of a distribution center and compare them to a typical return center in Exhibit A:

Exhibit A

Process Description	Distribution Center Operations	Return Center Operations
Inbound Receiving	You know what is coming in and verify receipts against PO's	No visibility to inbound receipts. Quantities & profiles unknown.
Receiving / Put Away	Location assigned by SKU / Cube / Velocity	Location assigned by return point, condition
Picking	By label / Pick-to-Light put on conveyor / cart/ pallet	By RMA / RA / BOL - picked by return point
Inventory	All SKU's in the facility are counted using cost	Only Inventory returned to Vendor / OEM
Shipping	Scheduled by order, by customer or store, on scheduled week days	Shipped by return authorization (RA) based on value / quantity / age
Thru Put / Productivity	Total Inbound Units + Outbound Units / Hours Worked	Total inbound units Received/ Hours Worked
Peak Season	October – December	December - March

As you can see from the table above, there are some fundamental differences. These differences are the result of underlying requirements of the business. For example, buyers will develop a merchandising plan, anticipate sales volumes, select manufacturers, schedule orders, and confirm deliveries that their supply chain executives use to for workload planning.

The Drivers Behind Returns

Returns are driven by the customer's buying patterns, returns patterns, conditions in the general economy, the release of new or replacement models, government action, and the quality of the goods purchased.

None of these drivers are known at any level of detail that would be useful when planning months or weeks in advance. As you can see, the basic underlying drivers behind a distribution network are clearly different than those of a returns network. These fundamental differences require different systems; different manpower planning tools; a different type of warehouse management; and different material handling equipment and processes.

A reverse logistics network is built primarily on three pillars that underpin every part the reverse logistics network. These pillars are those concrete parts of the business that force the requirements a company must live with, in order to effectively manage its reverse logistics pipeline. Once you understand these key foundational pillars, you can strategically address each of them to help improve customer satisfaction; maximize returned asset values; and improve relationships with key partners and vendors that support your business.

The first pillar that underpins a company's reverse logistics program is the company's published returns policy. A return policy defines the conditions required for the customer to return goods that they have purchased and want to return in exchange for new goods, cash, or credit. The policy's impact goes far beyond simply governing the transaction involving the return of an item. A return policy can define and in some cases, differentiate a company from its competitors or it can be the best method of advertising your competition will ever have. The return policy says more about a company's true dedication to customer service and how they see their position in the marketplace than virtually anything else.

The second pillar that provides the foundation for a quality reverse logistics program is the disposition guidelines and processes used to manage the disposition of returned assets. Disposition management is the act of identifying an asset, assessing its condition, and determining the best way to process the asset to maximize its net contribution to the company. Disposition management includes accounting processes; product segregation and grading processes; and preparation processes that may be required to efficiently and effectively prepare assets for their secondary market destination.

The third pillar of reverse logistics is the partnership agreements with suppliers. These agreements outline terms that delineate what product can be returned, liquidation arrangements with secondary market buyers, recycling procedures, and disposal guidelines. For many, the ability to control the secondary channel is critical to protecting their brand name, avoid litigation, and ensure regulatory compliance. Effective supplier agreements, as well as most liquidation agreements, clearly define product condition, terms of sales, and any associated restrictions on the final disposition of the product.

The Key to Bottom-Line Contributions

A company's structure and approach to supplier-partner agreements is the key to maximizing contributions from reverse logistics to the bottom line. These agreements are critical from a relationship-management standpoint between a company, its suppliers and its partners. Many companies diligently work to build strong relationships with their vendors during the sales process, only to see all that effort go up in smoke because of disputes over returns that could have been avoided by having a complete, well-thought-out agreement. Remember; return agreements are to suppliers and vendors what return policies are to customers. Both are equally important for manufacturers and retailers.

CHAPTER 2

The Most Important Decision

Many companies struggle with returns. Year after year, different leaders bemoan the level of returns and the uncontrollable costs associated with them. Some will throw a little money at the problem hoping for a quick, inexpensive fix. Not surprisingly, year after year, nothing changes.

For many, the only time the subject of returns management or reverse logistics arises is when a customer complains, suppliers balk, or the CFO reports a large write-down of returned inventory. When the CFO becomes involved, the focus is usually a debate centered on the obsolete and damaged inventory. Typically, the debate is concluded with a statement about how the inventory has to be written off to remain legally compliant. The financial impact is, of course, shockingly high and usually unbudgeted. Surprise!

Usually, these events are followed much hand wringing and talk about the need to do something. If the hue and cry gets loud enough or the financial surprise large enough, a cross-functional team is formed. This "action step" means for the next few months a select group of up and coming middle managers, who welcome the opportunity to stay late and work until midnight, will learn why no one in the organization has a clue about returns or how to permanently resolve the "returns problem."

The cross-functional team studies the problem, analyzes the data, and reads what little real information has been printed on the subject. Some call in outside vendors who, generally, shock them with costly solutions and lengthy time lines. The team speaks with industry peers who prove to be unknowledgeable about their own returns problems or have taken a vow of silence. Those who have worked in the reverse logistics industry long enough, can attest that industry surveys are notoriously vague and misleading, making the team's probing effort unhelpful.

In the end, this team of future senior leaders produces a report that has a few, weak recommendations that are made weaker by a lack of strong cost-benefit justification. In addition, while the team may have worked diligently on the project, they aren't comfortable enough to guarantee projected results. In fact, some team members position themselves to be well insulated from any further exposure to reverse logistics after the task force is disbanded. With that in mind, a report is issued that leads to little real action.

The following year, the CFO reports the amount of returned inventory written off and the cost of processing returns to the organization's leadership. This report is, inevitably, followed by more cries of pain and exasperation. The only difference is that, this time, somebody reminds the group that a cross-functional team was mobilized to address the issue. The team reported that, while everyone may be upset, the company was in the top fiftieth percentile in the industry and that overall; the organization's reverse logistics program is alive and well. Thus, the cycle is renewed and the problems remain unaddressed for yet another year.

THE MOST IMPORTANT DECISION

Returns Management—Corporately Cross-Cultural

The reason so many companies struggle with maximizing the effectiveness of their returns operations is that reverse logistics is corporately cross-cultural. Returns management not only crosses, but also blurs natural internal departmental boundaries. For example, in a retail environment, store operations must reverse the sales transaction when a customer returns an item. The buyer or merchandiser will take a margin hit when that same item is written off or marked down.

Transportation pays the cost to haul the item from the store. Warehouse operations pays for labor to unload, record, and store the item until it is disposed of, at which time the warehouse will for pay all the disposal costs. Along the reverse logistics pipeline, , no department is easily positioned to take responsibility to minimize the overall costs of handling the return---much less maximizing the value of the returned item upon disposal. Due to the nature of returns, from an organizational standpoint, there are traditional separations of duties and responsibilities that make managing returns challenging. Couple this with the fact that returns are generally an unpleasant challenge; you can see how reverse logistics can be the area of opportunity most often ignored in all types of companies.

For all of these real-world reasons, the first and most important decision a company can make to improve the management of returns is to put a senior leader in charge of returns management. This does not mean writing a returns management goal for the vice president of supply chain, or the CFO. This means making reverse logistics somebody's direct responsibility. For an organization to have an effective reverse logistics program, the organization must invest in leadership. You need someone waking up everyday worrying about one thing – turning that mess into profits; finding the hidden value in returns; improving customer service through effective returns management; becoming a better corporate citizen; and providing laser focused management of the returns process.

Curtis Greve's Walmart Experience

When I was first put in charge of returns operations at Walmart, Lee Scott, then vice-president of logistics and eventually Walmart's then chief executive officer (CEO), called and asked me to come over to his office. On the way over, I remember thinking he was going to give me a pep talk and tell me how important it was to provide great store service.

Much to my surprise, Lee wanted to talk to me about how important it was that I worked with the merchandising group and store operations. Lee told me he wanted me to attend the weekly merchandise meetings and work with store operations to develop store returns processes that would save the stores time and money. He expected me to develop programs to maximize the value of returns, improve vendor relations, and contribute to the bottom line. This was all on top of running great operations.

This was the first time I realized that I was responsible for more than just running a warehouse operation that happened to be called a return center. I was responsible for managing every aspect of reverse logistics in Walmart.

Lee wanted me to work with buyers on vendor agreement language, the invoice office task force on store processes, and work with the transportation department to ensure returns didn't utilize too many trailers that were needed to deliver new goods to stores that were serviced out of the local distribution center.

If a vendor was upset with the volume or condition of goods returned to them, it was my job to work with that vendor, merchandising, and store operations to develop a solution that worked for everyone. I remember driving home from the meeting thinking that this job was much bigger than I thought and feeling that I was probably underpaid.

Always the visionary and thought-leader, Lee Scott saw the value in the development of a comprehensive reverse logistics program. This program was to examine the reverse logistics problems from a cross-functional point of view and focused on opportunities for improvement.

Lucky for me, I was given the opportunity to focus all my time and energy on this effort. From 1988 to 1994, I was responsible for Walmart's reverse logistics program, spending much more of my time working with buyers, vendors, suppliers, store operations, systems, and accounting than I did managing the actual operation of the facility.

During this time, our effort increased return center productivity by one hundred and thirty percent. An amazing accomplishment! But the real impact on overall corporate profitability came from working with the related teams as directed by Lee Scott.

The true significance of this approach was recognized in 1990, when Mr. Walton requested that a special report on Walmart's returns program be included in the board of director's quarterly report.

As head of the program I benefitted from a unique, cross-cultural perspective that enabled me to assist various departments throughout Walmart to uncover opportunities and profits they might have overlooked or didn't realize existed. This unique perspective crosses internal functional boundaries that enable corporations to organizationally excel in their industries and add significant dollars to the bottom line. (8)

Leadership—The Key to Success

People are, as they are led. Without question, reverse logistics, like other functions of an organization, requires effective leadership. In fact, the Aberdeen Group study identified the establishment of an executive responsible for reverse logistics as a key success factor that all companies recognized as best in class shared. (6)

To be clear, establishing a leader responsible for reverse logistics does not mean that buyers, store operations, and warehouse operations report to that one "uber-leader." The head of an organization's reverse logistics program should be a well-respected person, with an appropriate level of experience, who is responsible for the direct expenses and the results of reverse logistics operations.

Most importantly, they must be capable of acting as an ambassador and facilitator with suppliers and, within all the organizations stakeholders, deliver real savings and maximize the corporate value received from world-class returns management.

Often, when this suggestion first arises, many CEOs and CFOs see this as another layer of bureaucracy and expense; they quickly discard the idea. However, the Aberdeen study discovered that the difference between reverse logistics program costs for best-in-class companies and their more poorly managed competitors was less than one percent of sales. (1)

Aberdeen also reported that the impact on earnings for best-in-class companies versus the more poorly managed companies was over five percent better in terms of total costs of returns. In addition, best-in-class customer satisfaction surveys averaged twelve percent higher. (1) It is clear that having an effective, best-in-class reverse logistics program is not dependent on spending more money. It is about spending the money in a proactive, more tightly focused manner that will produce the desired result. This goal can only be accomplished with strong, concerted leadership.

Consider the fact that for the average retailer in 2010, returns were a little over eight percent of sales. (5) Not assigning clear responsibility over reverse logistics is like a company ordering ninety-two percent of the products they are going to sell and then letting the suppliers "surprise" them with the remainder. Can you imagine that? Have you ever heard a buyer or purchasing agent say: "Eight percent? What the heck, it's not that much. Let the supplier pick the items and the price." Is this any different than allowing your company to manage reverse logistics by a blind committee that isn't held accountable for the results?

Establishing a person who is solely responsible for the development and maintenance of the reverse logistics program within an organization was a critical first step for Walmart in the 1980s. Today, it is still the most important step any company can take if they truly want to maximize the value that lies dormant within their reverse logistics operation.

To paraphrase that famous political quote: ***"It's leadership stupid!"*** Once a company has decided to put a competent, seasoned executive in charge of their reverse logistics program, the question of reporting becomes the next decision.

CHAPTER 3

Return Policies and Customer Satisfaction

According to an article written by J. Andrew Peterson and V. Kumar and published in the Spring 2010 edition of MIT Sloan Management Review, product returns cost companies over $100 billion or approximately 3.8 percent of profits every year. (10 page 85) note that the electronics industry spends over $14 billion on returns year. (Page 86)

When executives realize how returns impact sales, many will do what seems to come naturally and that is to reduce the volume of returns by tightening up their customer return policy. Many go so far as to institute anti-customer strategies such as restocking fees, reducing the time frame in which goods can be returned, or complicating the return authorization process. While these tactics may be effective in the short run, most of these measures have a detrimental impact on sales and are more costly than the product return over the long term.

In their study, Petersen and Kumar analyzed six years of customer purchases and subsequent returns for a nationally known catalogue retailer. (page 84) They found that a lenient return policy does NOT reduce profits but in fact promotes greater profits. They found that even with a higher return volume, the impact on the bottom line was positive. (page 85)

The Peterson-Kumar study results seem counter intuitive to what many think when looking at returns. Because of the huge financial impact of returns and the obvious impact on a company's bottom line, many companies attack the problem by restricting customer return privileges, which has been proven, time and again, not to work. In fact, this tactic is an unhealthy business practice. What many retailers find, much to their subsequent regret, is that when customer return privileges are restricted, in fact, sales are restricted, providing marketplace competitors a clear advantage.

Easing Return Policy – A Real World Example

In the fall of 2010, Best Buy realized that restricting returns did, in fact, have a negative impact on sales. This strategy drove Best Buy customers to its competitors. For a number of years, Best Buy had one of the most restrictive returns policies in the U.S. retail market. They would not accept some returns after specific time periods and would often charge restocking fees when purchases were retuned within the prescribed time after the initial sale. The result of this policy contributed to disappointing sales figures in November of 2010 and a warning about fourth quarter results that pulled the rug out from under their share price.

However, Best Buy didn't sit back and hope for miracle. Immediately following their poor numbers, they announced an easing of their customer return policy and eliminated many of their restocking fees. This all took place just a few days before Christmas of 2010. Best Buy's turn around on returns had a positive impact on customers, sales, and Best Buy's stock price. (7)

Customers responded positively to this easing of the return policy and purchased at Best Buy because the risk of making a bad purchase was limited. This is a clear illustration of the link between a company's return policy, their sales, and ultimately their marketplace value. (7)

Return Policies Limit Customer's Risk

To a customer, the return policy is really about limiting their risk. For the majority of buyers, the return policy is not about abusing the company they bought the product from. It is about spending money on an asset with some assurance that if the item does not satisfy their need for any reason, and the knowledge that they can return it and spend their money on a different item that will satisfy their need. If many executives looked at their return policies with this in mind, they would discard old return policies and rewrite them with their customers' needs, fears and concerns in mind.

The study conducted by Drs. Petersen and Kumar found that when return policies are less restrictive, customers tend to make more purchases because their risks are diminished. (10). The study also found that the returns process provides the seller with a critical opportunity to improve their relationship with their customers. (10) In fact, this study also found that the more a customer returns, the more they buy! (10)

There are two fundamental drivers behind every organization's return policy. First, it provides guidelines under which customers may return purchased items. Second, return policies describe the procedures that delineate what actions a company is willing to take to satisfy their customers.

Developing return policies is harder than you may think. Return policies are to companies what setting prices is to airlines. You don't want to be the first to make a restrictive change because it will likely cost you sales and customer share. Many companies have very complicated policies that confuse their customers and cause dissatisfaction. Others policies are very simple but poorly executed, which can also cause customer dissatisfaction.

Then there are those companies, such as Zappos, who have very liberal return policies, work hard to ensure that the customer returns experience is positive, and as a result, have a significant advantage in the marketplace.

It should be noted that return policies for shoes are much easier to write and administer than product categories such as high tech electronics, medical devices, control systems, or other complex industrial assets. For more complex assets and sales, more complex policies are required. These policies can include detailed warranty programs; variations on time windows; parts reimbursement; field services; and other features and services that can be very expensive.

Whether your return policy is simple or complex is only the first step toward satisfying your customers' returns needs. Just as important is how the policy is executed. Is the returns experience for your customer a positive or negative one?

If a retail store relaxes their return policy but does not focus on training their employees to be courteous to customers while interacting with them during the returns process, customers will not have a pleasant returns experience and will not be happy with that retail chain. Notice the word chain. Return policies and the returns process reflect on the entire organization, not just one store or one sales associate or one customer service representative. A positive experience reflects well on the whole company in the same way a negative one reflects poorly.

The Overall Returns Experience: A Critical Element

A study completed by Dr. Dale S. Rogers, then the head of the Supply Chain School at the University of Nevada Reno and now Professor, Logistics & Supply Chain Management at Rutgers University, found that if customers had a positive returns experience, they would return to shop at that store eighty-five percent of the time, whether they received a refund, exchange or nothing at all. (11)

Dr. Rogers also found that if the returns experience was not "good", ninety-five percent of the people surveyed said they would not shop at the store again, even if they received a refund. (11)

According to the Rogers survey, whether customers actually receive credit for a returned item or not, does not have as great an impact on how the customer viewed the company, as does the overall customer returns experience. (11) The "returns experience" is made up of two factors:

1. How are customers treated making the return or requesting authorization to make a return? Customers must always be treated with respect and empathy.
2. The returns policy itself, whether strict or not, does not seem to matter. What matters is that the details of the return policy are clear, easy to understand, and consistently communicated to the customer.

Published Return Policies

Read the following excerpts from the return policies of leading manufacturers and retailers and think about how they might impact you as a potential customer.

"Satisfaction Guaranteed or Your Money Back"

"You can return or exchange in-store purchases at any location. Bring the original receipt and your photo ID. A restocking fee may be applied in some product categories."

"Most store items can be exchanged or refunded with a receipt within 90 days of purchase. "

"Items must be returned within 90 days and must be in new and unused condition and contain all original packaging and accessories."

"Our goal is that you are completely satisfied with your purchase. We take pride in the quality of the products we sell and offering great customer service is our top priority. If you are not completely satisfied with your purchase, please follow the guidelines detailed below and we will be happy to help you to return your purchase."

"Our ultimate goal is for you to be completely satisfied with your purchase. If you receive an item you are dissatisfied with, you may return it within ninety (90) days to any store for a refund or exchange within our current return policy guidelines."

"You can return or exchange your purchase to any store or by mail. Plus, you have 180 days to decide!"

"We guarantee your satisfaction on every product we sell with a full refund. The following must be returned within 90 days of purchase for a refund: televisions, projectors, computers, cameras, camcorders, iPod / MP3 players and cellular phones."

"You may return most new, unopened items sold and fulfilled within 30 days of delivery for a full refund. We'll also pay the return shipping costs if the return is a result of our error. Items should be returned in their original product packaging."

"You may return any or all of your merchandise for any reason within 30 days of purchase.

[if you are quoting these policies verbatim from different companies, and it sounds like you are (that's why I left the numbers as is) then you have to cite where each came from parenthetically after each one like this: (Walmart) (Target) If there is a page number that can be noted then it should look like this: (Kmart, 254) Then, in the bibliography, you have to include the source from whence each one came. If you got it from their website, then you have to use the MLA citation for a website. If you wrote it down while standing in line at the check out…well, I'll have to look that one up.]

Complete the following exercise. The exercise is simple and will only take a few minutes but could have a significant impact on your organization.

1. Read your organization's return policy. Put yourself in the shoes of your customer. Does your policy seem ambiguous? Is your return policy customer-friendly or does is it position your customer as an adversary?
2. Read your top three competitors' return policies, (these can typically be found on the Internet).
3. Compare and contrast your company's return policy with those of your competitors. Does your policy provide a competitive advantage or disadvantage? Will it help or hurt sales and profits?

Often, return policies appear to have been written by the vice-president of **sales prevention**. Return policies are clearly one important differentiator used by customers when making a purchase decision. The question is whether a return policy is a positive differentiator that improves customer satisfaction or is it a wedge between your company and your customer.

Realize that the vast majority of your customers, NEVER read your company's returns policy until they want or need to return an item. This is when customer satisfaction can be enhanced or destroyed. Remember the Aberdeen Group study found that a company's returns process could impact customer satisfaction by **twelve percent** or more. Not only will your company's ability to provide a positive customer experience in the return process improve customer satisfaction, it will do significant harm to your organization's reputation and sales growth, if the experience is negative. Most customers who have a negative returns experience will not only NOT buy from you again but will also tell other potential customers who may have been thinking about making a purchase from your company to NOT buy from you.

The Reason for Returns Is Customer Satisfaction

Reverse logistics was born out of the desire to improve customer satisfaction. As competition increased and the living standard improved after World War II, customers demanded better quality and service. As a result, people started to return items at a greater rate. Retailers and manufacturers, seeing an opportunity to gain or keep market share, eased their return policies. For many companies, such as Walmart, the return policy was way to differentiate themselves to their customers

A Real-Life Returns Story

In the mid 1980's, when I was responsible for Walmart's reverse logistics program, I received a call from Sam Walton's office. Mr. Sam requested that I send him a returned item that represented an outrageous example of an item that had been returned, and money refunded, to a customer in violation of our return policy. He was going to use it at an upcoming store manager's meeting. I went out on the return center floor and found a Stanley Thermos that had recently been received from a store. On the bottom of the thermos there was a date stamped showing the date of manufacture - **1954**. The first Walmart store didn't open until **1962**. I grabbed the thermos and the store return tag and sent it to Mr. Sam's office.

A few weeks later, at the Walmart Store Manager's meeting, Mr. Sam held the thermos up and asked the store manager that had given the refund to come up on stage. The nervous manager walked up on stage and stood beside Mr. Sam, in front of thousands of fellow store managers, district managers, and support staff. Each person in the audience was incredibly glad not to be that poor guy.

Mr. Sam raised the very thermos I had sent to his office and praised the store manager for doing such a great job of serving his customers. Mr. Sam shook his hand, told everyone to give the man a round of applause, and then talked about the importance taking care of the customer. In fact, Mr. Sam was effusive in his praise of the store manager standing beside him. It went on for at least ten minutes. Soon, everyone in the crowd was envious of this manager who was now about six inches taller than when he walked up on stage.

Mr. Sam wanted everyone to know that this manager understood that taking back a return wasn't about a thermos. It was about customer satisfaction. The returned thermos may have cost Walmart twenty dollars in the short run, but that happy customer the returns experience created was worth thousands of dollars over their life as a happy Walmart customer.

All the Walmart store managers in the attendance got the message. Over the next few months, the volume of Walmart returns increased significantly, as did sales, earnings, and market share. —all a direct result of **keeping customers happy, one return at a time.** By the way, that same Stanley thermos is now on display in Walmart's Visitor's Center in Bentonville Arkansas. The message lives on today.(8)

Reverse logistics is all about customer satisfaction. Customer satisfaction may not always start with returns or a return policy but it certainly can end there. The Aberdeen Group study cites that out of the one hundred sixty enterprises examined, those companies ranked in the top twenty percent--- in terms of the quality of their reverse logistics program--- had an average customer satisfaction rating of ninety-three percent. Comparatively, firms ranked in the lower eighty percent had a customer satisfaction rating of eighty-one percent---a twelve percent difference in satisfaction. (1)

Interestingly, the same study found that for both, the top twenty and lower eighty percent, the cost of reverse logistics, as a percent of total sales was within one percent. (1) The key point being, it isn't about spending more money to process returns. The difference is in how and where you invest the money in your reverse logistics program.

The gross amount of returns is often a metric closely tracked by a company's leadership team. All too often management looks at returns only in the context of fraud and abuse by their customers, and not as an opportunity to improve customer relations. Fraud and abuse is often thought to be a big issue in returns management. A study completed by the National Retail Federation in 2009 found that fraud and abuse accounts for only eight percent of all returns, which is 0.6% of total sales. (13) Clearly this is still a significant amount of money. Management and loss prevention must do what they can to reduce fraud and abuse. However, a company's return policy should be written for the majority of honest, non-abusive customers who just want to be treated fairly, not for the less than one percent of customers who abuse the system.

If a company can improve their customers' perceptions of their returns policy and process by improving the way the return policy is written and how customers are treated during the returns process; customer satisfaction will surly improve. As this occurs, sales will grow, customer turnover will decrease, employee moral will improve, and earnings will go up. There is a direct, undeniable relationship between customer satisfaction and a company's return policy. Whether it is a high tech firm, online retailer, industrial manufacturer, major department store, or a local grocer, the organization's execution of its return policy is a daily demonstration of how much the company values long-term customer loyalty and to what extent the company will go to create, nurture and cherish it.

CHAPTER 4

The Key To Increasing

Recovery Rates

In order to more fully understand excellence in reverse logistics and sustainability, an executive must grasp one of the most important concepts: disposition management. Disposition management is the key to maximizing the value of assets flowing through an organization's reverse logistics pipeline. The term "disposition management" refers to the process of identifying, inspecting, sorting, processing, and shipping returned products, as well as processing the related financial transactions. This is all done in accordance with predetermined agreements between the buyer and seller of that specific asset, and based on the condition of that specific, unique item in the reverse logistics pipeline.

Perhaps the best way to explain disposition management is to use a fairly common example. First, you must understand a key difference in the handling requirements of a distribution facility versus a returns facility. Just for the record, this example applies to any returns process, whether the returns processing function is centralized or not.

A distribution center receives items by SKU, UPC, model number, or some other form of unique identifier assigned to that item. The item comes in a the same size box, in new condition, and is generally put in the same area of the warehouse where it is picked and shipped according to order requirements. There is typically little or no variation from one unit of the same SKU to the next unit. The red balls always go in location "X", are picked by the full case, and shipped to the store or customer, packed and delivered in the normal manner. Red balls are handled the same way today that they were yesterday and will be handled that way tomorrow.

Processing by Disposition

Returns processing is quite different. For example, in a return center, items are received by SKU, UPC, model number, or some other unique item identifier. However, each individual item is then inspected and the profile of that item is determined. The "return profile" of an item denotes its cosmetic condition, functionality, components, age, reason for return, and other general characteristics of that specific item. After each individual item has been profiled, the product is sorted by item and profile. These different sorts are shipped to different locations and each sort type can have a dramatically different financial impact on the company processing that returned item.

For example, a retail return facility receives a pallet with six flat screens televisions. Each of the televisions is the same size and all are the same SKU and model number. The first is brand new. In fact, it was a special order for Christmas but did not sell. The packaging has never been opened but there is a big Christmas tree on the side of the box. When the manufacturer sold the television to the retail buyer, a commitment was made by the manufacturer to take back any unsold items that are in the special Christmas packaging for full cost credit plus transportation costs and a handling or consolidation fee. As a result, the first television is sorted as a "recall" and shipped back to the manufacturer for full cost plus a consolidation fee. In the reverse logistics world, a consolidation fee is the same as a handling fee.

Upon inspecting the second television on the pallet, it is determined that it was sold to and returned by a customer who said it "didn't work". Upon further investigation, according to the serial number and the attached receipt, the item was sold fewer than ninety days ago. This television is unboxed. The return center operations team, plugs the set in, tests it by running the manufacturer's suggested diagnostic package, and ensures that all of the original components are present. The inspection found no faults and the television seems to be in perfect condition, other than the open packaging. This item was probably returned due to "buyer's remorse which is a politically correct way of saying "my wife got really mad when she found out how much I paid for this thing and I have to get my money back or get a lawyer."

In this example, we are going to assume that the terms of the vendor agreement that governs returns clearly address this type of return and the retailer is not allowed to return items that passed the operational test. With this condition, the item is repackaged and will be sold, "as is", on the retailer's business –to-consumer (B2C) web site for eighty percent of normal retail cost.

The third television looks like it has been run over by a truck. The glass screen is broken, the frame is cracked in three places, and there is no way this item can be repaired. An item in this condition can't be returned because it is a clear case of customer abuse. In this scenario, the unit would be taken to the recycling area where useable parts are salvaged for the repair of other units. The remaining pieces that can be recycled, are recycled. What can't be recycled or used in the repair process is thrown in the dumpster. In this situation, this television is a complete loss and the retailer hopes to break even between the value of saving parts, recycling, and the cost of disposal.

The fourth television coming off of this pallet to be processed appears to be in good working order but it is about two years old and clearly beyond the return terms agreed to with the manufacturer. The retailer will place this unit on a bulk liquidation pallet, where it will be shipped to a buyer who will pay twenty-five percent of wholesale cost for "as is" consumer electronic products. There are two options for most companies when it comes to product of this type. First, you can repair the item, if necessary, and sell it at a higher recovery rate or you can sell it "as is", and in both cases, sell the product directly to the end consumer (B2C), or to a bulk liquidator business-to-business. (B2B) We will address the differences between these secondary market options later in this book.

The fifth television looks fine, but it fails diagnostic checks. There is something wrong and it is deemed "defective". This item is will be sent back to the manufacturer for full cost credit, plus a handling or consolidation fee. This is similar to the seasonally recalled item discussed above, however, televisions in this category are shipped to different locations and the consolidation fee for the defect unit is higher than the fee charged for the recalled unit. NOTE: The standard default basis for cost of returned goods, or any asset processed through a reverse channel is last cost in the system. There are some exceptions for special-order merchandise, but for the most part, the last cost in the system of the processor is used for all transactional calculations.

The final television on the pallet to be processed is over ninety days old, passes all tests, but has a significant scratch on the screen that won't buff out. The liquidators will only pay fifteen percent of cost for flat screen television with a scratched screen. The huge discount the secondary market will want for a unit with this cosmetic issue coupled with the high cost to replace the glass, does not warrant repair of the item. However, the local Catholic Charities Home for Unwed Mothers will take the item with a smile and the retailer can write off the retail value of the television off as a charitable donation. The Home for Unwed Mothers is delighted. The retailer gets a tax benefit, the satisfaction of helping the needy and achieving a sustainability goal of keeping usable items in use for as long as possible.

This process of inspecting and sorting the same item by condition and profile compared to a predetermined set of guidelines, as in this example, is effective disposition management. Consider the huge variation in the value of the returned item based on the disposition management rules that are established for this single television SKU. At the high end of the spectrum, the item will result in a full cost credit plus a higher handling fee. At the low end, the retailer not only had to write the item off, but also had to pay to have parts of the unit disposed of in a landfill.

Improve Disposition Values

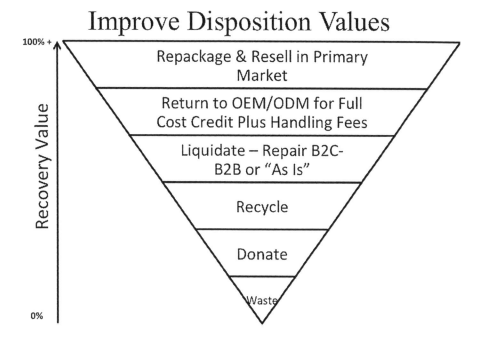

The variation of disposition avenues and their related financial consequences impact the decision-making process. The expert management of these variations is what separates the best-in-class reverse logistics operations from their competitors. In simple terms, it is the difference between having to write off the item completely, and the cost of disposal--- versus averaging a total recovery rate of eighty to ninety percent plus handling fees that can range from one to ten percent of the value of the asset processed. In the 1970s and 1980s most companies simply destroyed these returned products by sending all returns that could not be put directly back on the shelf to landfills. Today, companies can dramatically impact not only their bottom line but reduce the amount of usable product that pollutes our environment and save landfill fees in the process.

When you first look at disposition management, it seems very complicated and challenging. At a certain level of detail, disposition management can be complicated. If a company has a significant number of SKU's the sum of the total can be challenging to say the least. Many companies, however, are surprised to learn that, regardless of whether you are returning a can of soup, a big screen television, a $25,000 server, or a ten dollar doll, there are, ultimately, only six different dispositions for any returned item.

Regardless of the item returned, it will be returned to the original manufacturer, returned to stock, sold on the secondary market, recycled, donated to charity, or disposed of in a landfill or incinerator. That is it. The most important part of a reverse process is how the process sorts returned assets into these six dispositions. While there are only six primary disposition sorts, there are numerous variations that can have a significant financial impact on a company, but eighty percent of the value of a reverse logistics process is derived from getting assets in the right disposition bucket.

The Reverse Logistics Process Flow

The following Reverse Logistics Process Flow illustrates a typical scenario of item flow. From a financial perspective, the customer is credited when the item is returned. When the company receives the item they take ownership. The price of taking this ownership is usually the original sales price. Which, when applied internally, puts the asset on the books at the original cost.

The process on the left side of the chart below shows the flow of goods that coincide with this transfer of ownership back from the customer. The right side of the chart is the process where, financially, the "residual value" of the returned asset is realized and the cost of processing is incurred.

That residual value could range from zero to full recovery of the cost of the item, plus appropriate processing or handling fees. This illustrates how "dispositioning" drives the value realization of the reverse logistics process.

While this chart shows the disposition of goods flowing into shipping, the terms of shipping and the destination of the actual goods vary greatly. There are many factors that determine which party pays for shipping and where the product movement terminates. Usually, it's a matter of negotiation between the buyer and seller when the initial purchase is made. There is not one set rule that governs this aspect of the process.

Reverse Logistics Process Flow

While there are no set rules or guidelines that can be applied to every agreement governing returns and recalls, there are some helpful industry-wide best practices that one can use to as a starting point for negotiations, including:

- The manufacturer / OEM generally pays for freight directly or indirectly for returned assets, whether defective or recalled.
- Retailers typically deduct the cost of returns, including charges for inventory, processing, and freight from any outstanding payables they have with the manufacturer.
- Liquidators, meaning buyers of product on the secondary market, generally provide their own transportation or pay for shipper-arranged transportation.
- Typically, high tech, market-dominant manufacturers will not pay consolidation or handling fees and will be much more strict in negotiating the terms and conditions for returned product.

- Goods returned by retailers that do not comply with previously agreed-to terms and conditions are generally not returned, nor credited in any way.
- Manufacturers of commodities will pay handling fees but will expect compliance and support where customer abuse is evident.

Often, offshore Original Equipment Manufacturers (OEMs) have no place to receive and process returns. These OEMs will often agree to allow retailers to liquidate their product AND give credit for the cost value of the returned product. They generally don't pay handling fees but liquidation revenue is much higher so it is a win/win.

Consolidation and Handling Fees

Consolidation or handling fees are paid as a percentage of wholesale cost or a flat dollar amount, per unit, for higher priced items. The basis for the consolidation fees should be to cover the cost of processing returns, not including transportation.

Disposal fees are passed on directly to OEMs when required by the manufacturer. This is especially true if assets have to be incinerated or disposed of in a hazardous materials landfill. Disposal fees are NOT passed on for private-label goods or product that the retailer or business destroys for brand protection reasons.

As stated earlier, all these terms are negotiable so use this list as a baseline when working out return privileges. In later chapters, many of these topics will be explored in-depth. For now, this is a good list to start with to build or improve your reverse logistics program.

The chart below shows the profit and loss impact by disposition along with the average percentage of total volume for a typical mass merchant's merchandise mix.

Typical Mass Merchandise Retailer's Disposition by Inventory Mix

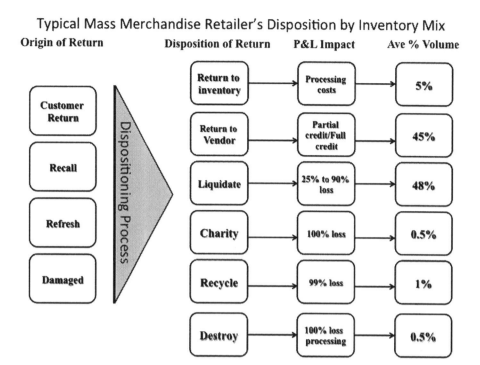

CHAPTER 5

Outsourcing Reverse Logistics

The first known instance of outsourcing dates back to the book of Genesis, Chapter 38, when a eunuch of the Pharaoh, Potiphar, outsourced his back office and support functions to a soon to be famous service-provider named Joseph. Later, after a contract dispute, Joseph ended up in prison. But Joseph was a man of dreams and vision, which landed him the job of prisoner management.

This proved to be a wise move. Joseph's expertise, low overhead, singular focus, and attention to detail significantly improved productivity and the customer eagerly recommended Joseph to others who were considering outsourcing.

It should be noted that this was the first time Joseph was tapped for his best-in-class leadership. Later, as a result of Joseph's ability to provide visibility; quality management information; inspired regression analysis; and long-term strategic planning; Pharaoh out-sourced to Joseph warehousing; distribution, and, later, all back-of-fice support functions. In this way, the outsourcing of supply chain functions was born. Companies around the world have been adopt-ing this strategy ever since.

Today, companies outsource for many of the same reasons that Pharaoh did thousands of years ago. Companies outsource primarily for one of three reasons:

1. The company does not have the internal expertise and needs an outside firm that has a proven core competency in the area of need.
2. The company wishes to achieve greater flexibility and faster speed to market.
3. The company desires a protective barrier against outside forces and limit potential liabilities.

Many of the world's largest companies outsource internal functions, as mentioned above, because they do not have the expertise within their management ranks to operate the function, or they don't elect to use available resources on the function under consideration.

This is often the case with returns management and reverse logistics. Few companies want to assign top talent to returns pro-cessing. Retailers need their top executives working on ways to improve traditional, core supply-chain functions, or store operations, or merchandising systems. Manufacturers, for the same reasons, want their top talent running manufacturing plants, working with customers, managing imports, or managing parts---just about any-thing other than focusing on returns. Returns are, more often than not, treated like the red-headed stepchild of the company. No one wants to deal with returns.

When I first got involved with returns and before I would agree to the responsibility, Lee Scott, my supervisor at that time had to prom-ise me that I would not have to spend any more than two years in returns before he would assign me to a distribution center leader-ship position. That was twenty-five years ago. I am still dealing with returns. (8)

Why Outsource Returns

The point is that returns management and reverse logistics are often outsourced because there is no internal expertise and few companies give it the priority it needs to garner the resources needed to maximize the opportunity.

This is why the majority of retailers and manufacturers who don't simply ignore returns, outsource their returns processing functions. A qualified third-party logistics provider * (3PL) can have a significant impact on a company simply because of their experience in returns.

They can also help the hiring company leapfrog the competition by leveraging systems, liquidation networks, and sharing best operations practices to reduce the cost of processing.

The key, however, is to outsource to a firm that is experienced and has a broad view of the issues. Many 3PLs claim they "process returns", but few actually do. Fewer still has any idea about what happens upstream or downstream from the actual returns processing function and how they must be coordinated to achieve maximum results.

Another Walmart Story

The best explanation I've ever heard on the value of experience came from Charlie Self who was the controller of Walmart when I was an internal auditor, which was my first job out of college. It was June 1983. At that time, Sam Walton was a local hero who was a fairly well-known leader of a midsized retailer based in Bentonville, Arkansas. There were about four hundred Walmart stores. The company was just starting to get national attention.

The Director of Internal Audit, Dave Gorman, hired me. For some reason, he decided to take a chance on hiring a mediocre accounting student from Arkansas Tech University. I've often thought that, had I applied ten years later, I would not have gotten an interview. In any event, roughly a year later, Dave Gorman was promoted to vice president of loss prevention. This was big move for Dave and all nine

---

* These are companies that manage warehousing, transportation, and any related functions.

of us in the internal audit department were proud of our former boss. There was a bit of a sibling rivalry between the internal audit and loss prevention departments and promoting somebody from our department to oversee our rivals gave us reason to puff out our chests a bit.

For the next year or so, the Internal Audit Department's Assistant Director, Joe Moore, took over the helm. Joe was a "good old boy"---an ex-store manager whose real expertise was in scheduling and conducting store inventories. Why, he didn't even have an accounting degree. In fact, he didn't really like doing audits.

Those facts bothered me, and some of the other young guns who clearly knew more about auditing than Joe--- or so we thought. What we didn't know, however, was that Joe was a great servant-leader. He served as an interim director only because he wanted to maintain a life-balance between job and family. Joe had turned down the permanent position.

As time passed with our "interim leader", I became more concerned about the lack of development, drive, and strategic focus of the department. I could see Dave Gorman driving the loss prevention department. What was once a source of pride in his accomplishments was becoming a source of envy for what he was achieving with our rival department.

I thought it was time for action. I called Charlie Self, who was directly responsible for the internal audit department and requested a meeting to discuss departmental leadership. Charlie was the longtime head of finance and accounting for Walmart. He was a respected voice on Wall Street, and about five levels my senior. At the time I was too stupid to understand that it was not appropriate for a young guy in an entry-level position to actually meet with the man who typically only spoke to stock analysts on the phone---that was by appointment only.

As far as I was concerned, Charlie was simply the man who would hire the next director of internal audit. He was very polite and set up a time the next day for us to meet, in his office. This says much about the Walmart culture. It is because of leaders like Charlie Self and Lee Scott that Walmart is what it is today.

The next day I went to his office, which was three doors down from Sam Walton's office. I strode into executive row like I belonged there and knew my way around. I'm sure the executive assistants were snickering as I walked down the hallway of death---fat, dumb and happy. What I was doing?

I knocked on the door and Charlie invited me in. I thanked him for taking the time to see me, and proceeded to tell him that I realized that the directorship of my department was a position crucial to our success. We needed to permanently fill it with a leader who would continue to develop our programs and help drive Walmart to be the best retail chain in history. (I had practiced my first five lines at least twenty times the night before.)

I then, humbly, offered up my services to fill the position. I was twenty-three years old. I knew that I would be the youngest director in the history of Walmart. But I was hoping that my age and inexperience were offset by my extraordinarily strong work ethic and ambition. Honestly, I can't remember exactly what I said, but that was the gist of it.

What I do remember, clearly, was the smile that came across Charlie's face. He asked me to sit down, much like an uncle who is getting ready to teach you an important lesson. Charlie then asked me a few questions that changed how I looked at leaders for the rest of my life.

"Who do you think is the highest paid person at Walmart?" Charlie asked in a slow, gentle tone.

"Why, I would say David Glass." I said. David had just been promoted to CEO and reported to Mr. Walton, who was then chairman of the board.

"Correct!" Charlie said. "And why do you think Sam pays David more than anyone else?" he continued.

After a few seconds of trying to come up with some reason that made sense I said: "Well, he is the CEO."

"Does he know more about store operations than anyone?" Charlie asked.

"No, I'm sure Jack Shoemaker knows more about operations," I said. Jack Shoemaker was widely praised as the best store operator in the country and was the president of Walmart during its meteoric rise to national prominence.

"Correct, he does. Jack's the best, clearly better than David. Does David know more about merchandising than anyone?" Charlie asked.

"The best merchant according to Mr. Walton is Bill Fields," I said.

"I would have to agree with that," Charlie said. "How about finance, do you think David knows more about accounting and finance than Jimmy Walker or me?" he queried.

Jimmy was known to be "the man" when it came to all things accounting and I was smart enough not to insult Charlie. "No, I'm sure Jimmy knows more and I'm sure you know more than Jimmy," I replied.

"Right again," Charlie said. "So why does David Glass make more than anyone else in the company if he isn't the best at anything?" Charlie asked.

I sat back in my chair, realizing I failed the test. "I really don't know sir," I sighed. My rocket ride to the top was quickly coming back to earth.

"Let me tell you," Charlie said with a smile. "David Glass has had a lot of experiences working for Walmart and other companies. He is the very best at learning from those experiences and applying those lessons to current and future events." Charlie sat back in his chair and went on: "David is a great leader. He listens, thinks, applies his lessons from his experience, and helps us avoid many problems and ensures we make the most of our opportunities."

I started to get it.

To this day, I still see Charlie's face when he told me this. David Glass was the best at being a good leader. It wasn't his ability to run a store, or pick an item, or balance an account that made him worth more than anyone else at Walmart. It was his ability to learn from his experiences and apply them to future events that enabled Walmart to avoid problems and make the most of its opportunities.

In the famous Saturday morning meetings at Walmart, David Glass was known for correcting people when they would say something like, "that is a problem". David would say "You mean that is an opportunity". That is what great leaders do. They help everyone see the opportunities.

Sam Walton, David Glass, Jack Shoemaker, Lee Scott---all kept their eyes on their goals. They were great leaders not because of their great speaking ability, or knowledge of a particular discipline, but because they learned from their experiences and helped their teams take advantage of that same experience. Additionally, they were great at seeing beyond the obstacles and were able to teach their teams to believe that they could overcome.

Charlie had pointed out that to be a good leader; you really do need more than just drive and dedication. You need experience---experience that you have learned from. That's what a great leader brings to the table.

As you can probably guess, I didn't get the promotion. However, I did get a valuable lesson in leadership from a senior vice president of a Fortune 500 company who was happy to take the time to teach a kid a few things they don't cover in school.

As for the position, it was filled by a guy from J.C. Penney named Jim Kent. He had a lot of experience. Jim was very intelligent and, as it turned out, was one of the most inspiring leaders that I had the pleasure of working with. Jim went on to fill many leadership positions and so did I---in large part, thanks to the lessons Jim taught me.

Today, my business is based on helping people learn from my experience. I hope Charlie is smiling and proud of the lessons I learned at his knee. (8)

Selecting and 3PL

Selecting a 3PL, it is all about the experience. Can they help you improve the product flow upstream so you can process more efficiently and maximize the value of the returned assets downstream? Do they understand the impact of returns on customers, suppliers, stores, and distribution centers, as well as how they affect the financial well-being of the company?

Lack of on-point experience is often why companies outsource reverse logistics; but speed and flexibility also drive many to outsource. Often, companies outsource reverse supply chain functions, not because they don't have the leadership or experience, but because they need a solution fast. Hiring a 3PL with the focus, motivation, experience, existing technology, capital resources, and staff brings operations live much faster than the outsourcer could on its own.

A critical factor in selecting a 3PL is its facility start-up expertise and bench-strength management. These factors effectively enable a 3PL to move quickly and start operations within a matter of weeks. In fact, it is not uncommon for a first tier 3PL to get an operation up and running within ninety days. Typically, an outsourcer's capital approval process alone takes much longer than ninety days.

The third reason companies outsource supply chain functions, including reverse logistics, is to have a layer of protection and minimize their risk. Many companies outsource operations to avoid unwanted attention from labor unions.

Why Outsource to a Third-party

It is against U.S. law for a company to fire employees who attempt to organize a labor union. However, a company can fire a 3PL and replace them with another if the first doesn't meet performance metrics. This is true even if the 3PL does not achieve its goals because of a strike or other union activities.

Companies also outsource to cap or better-control certain risks such as inventory shrinkage, workers compensation expenses, medical benefit costs, or other "non-controllable" expenses. Companies protect themselves by either negotiating a fixed-fee arrangement for multiple years or with some form of variable pricing. Either outsourcers pay a fee that is based, in part, on these expenses or they have their upside risk for these categories capped. Often, contracts allow for the sharing of any savings derived from the partnership.

When I was working for a 3PL, part of my job was to be the primary customer liaison with senior executives from our biggest customers. One customer shared that the only reason he decided to outsource operations to our company was because, as a 3PL, we would effectively provide a cap on workers' compensation costs for the operation He clearly understood the financial ramifications of outsourcing. He viewed the fee paid to the 3PL as an insurance policy that capped workers' compensation and insulated his company from inventory shrinkage, employee lawsuits, and other risks. (8)

The outsourcing of returns management and other supply chain functions continues to grow and has outpaced gross domestic product (GDP) growth for the last twenty years. (11) While on a relative basis, the growth in outsourcing is slowing slightly; corporations around the world continue to look to outsourcing as a means to improve overall performance.

A strong, new trend is evidenced when a plethora of buzzwords develop just to describe it. Prior to the late 1980s, the term 3PL did not even exist!

Today many don't know what 3PL that stands for. For the newbie's it stand for Third Party Logistics Providers.

Trends in Outsourcing

Warehouse operators and transportation companies are the main benefactor of the outsourcing trend. But over the past twenty years, no industry has benefited more than 3PLs. At its origin, third-party logistics was an industry rooted in hometown warehouse owners and small regional carriers that were forced to adapt to a world of deregulated, systems-driven, non-asset based practices. Many 3PLs began as companies that owned a warehouse in a key geographic location. As deregulation took hold and manufacturing consolidated and moved off shore, the surviving companies took advantage of opportunities to expand services.

Those 3PLs that embraced the future, invested in technology, and altered their models thrived. Those that stubbornly held on to old value propositions have gone by the wayside. In fact, this dichotomy produced significant mergers and acquisition activity in the 3PL space.

In the current market, (spring 2010) there are three major groups of 3PLs. There is a handful of very large companies with revenues in the billions. There is a large number of smaller providers with revenues under $250 million. And then, there are firms situated in the middle of these two groups which tend to either be acquired by the "big boys" or slowly lose customers and become irrelevant, shrinking their way to the lower tier of providers. All are trying to expand their service offerings and, interestingly, increase the cost of change for their customers. That is to say, 3PLs try to provide so many integrated services that it is more costly for a customer to change providers than it could ever be worth to do so.

Cost of Change

Understanding "the cost of change" is critical to organizations that are outsourcing or are considering changing service providers. While outsourcing supply chain management continues to grow, competition between 3PLs is increasing as well. Many who have outsourced for years are now seeing the power of competition. Companies often use two or more 3PLs when they can and one for their entire network. Executives tasked with the responsibility of managing 3PL relationships are getting smarter and negotiating tougher terms.

3PLs find themselves in the unenviable position of having to bid on business that they have had for years, knowing that their best-case scenario is to retain the business at a lower margin. Many retailers and manufacturers require a request for proposal (RFP) process that doesn't place any value on past performance or loyalty on the part of the incumbent. With the proliferation of systems across the spectrum of supply chain functions, more and more providers find their services and the associated value commoditized. Most 3PL executives see requirements getting tighter, competition getting tougher, and margins getting squeezed. One of a 3PL's greatest challenges is to find ways to keep themselves from being treated as a commodity. Finding a specialized niche or service that sets them apart from their competition is key.

Today, every 3PL is looking for methods, services, and products that will increase their margin and the cost of change for their customers. In this way, 3PLs may be able to get off the RFP merry-go-round and bring a semblance of stability to their profits.

For example, if you were a customer of a bank and used their online services for years, then decided to change banks, there would be an additional cost of change for the extra time and trouble experienced in shutting down one account and opening another. You would have to get set up on your new bank's systems. Learn their online features. Set up all of your bills for automatic payment. All of this is already in place at your old bank. You may not have considered the value of this effort when comparing the price between the two banks

In the world of outsourcing, the cost of switching from one provider to another can be very expensive, disruptive to your business, negatively impact your customers directly, and in some cases, not even be possible until the end of a contract. Many service providers work very hard to get their customers to buy software, use supporting services such as transportation management; invoice processing; call center operations; refurbishing and repair services; kitting; packaging; parts management; liquidation services; and much more just to make it more complex and costly to unplug. These ancillary services typically are priced with a higher margin. This may sound underhanded but it really isn't. Third-party logistics providers invest significant time, energy, and money to develop and maintain an operation. If start-up costs are not factored into the pricing, the service provider often does not actually make a profit until the final year of a contract.

In addition, losing a customer is really hard on a service provider. Not only do they lose the revenue but also often have to lay people off, terminate good employees, and incur substantial shut-down costs that may not be reimbursed. In the end, 3PLs work to ensure that their customers appreciate the services they provide and are as loyal to the service provider as the service provider is to them.

3PLs Try to Increase Cost of Change

Many supply chain companies are working to increase the cost of change by developing reverse logistics capabilities. If you are a 3PL executive who is considering this, there are a few things you need to keep in mind. First, the priorities in reverse logistics are completely different than normal forward logistics. Timing, for example, is not as critical as having the ability to profile each individual SKU as it comes into the warehouse. Every item can be handled one of six ways, as we discussed in the chapter on disposition management. You must know how to determine the disposition and what characteristics drive that disposition.

Depending on the market you are targeting, returns processing could require a basic understanding of repair techniques, parts management, liquidation, and recycling. The degree of each requirement depends on your customer and the category of product you will handle.

Warehouse Management Software Systems Don't Work In Reverse

Your existing warehouse management software (WMS) will not work in reverse. Often, supply chain executives wrongly decide that processing mostly damaged or obsolete product does not require good leadership and specialized systems. Warehouse management software providers want you to believe that their system will work in reverse. Do not believe it.

Would you use a transportation system to run a warehouse? Would you use a warehouse management system to run the cash registers in a store? Don't try to use a WMS system to process returns. You must have a reverse logistics software (RLS) package to effectively manage the product flow and disposition of returned goods. You will also need great leadership that is knowledgeable about your customers' businesses and committed to improve your customers' bottom lines, not just yours. Many of the brightest supply chain minds in the world have tried to take shortcuts on returns management and their companies have always paid the price.

If you ever have a doubt about justifying the investment in specialized returns management software, facilities, leadership, or processes, just remind yourself that on average 8% of all inventory that is sold is returned; and processing those returns can cost your company between 9% and 15% of sales. What other part of your organization has this size of impact---but is totally ignored or neglected?

Should 3PLs Develop Reverse Logistics

Does the development of reverse logistics capabilities make financial sense for most 3PLs? It depends on the individual 3PL. For the most part, fees in the reverse world can be as much as twenty to forty percent higher than traditional distribution and transportation services. It really boils down to the needs of your customer base, your internal capacity to take on the task of developing new services and your appetite for investing in a development process that may not see any real profits for eighteen to twenty-four months.

If done correctly, developing reverse logistics capabilities can work for both the service provider and the customer that owns the returned product. However, in order to achieve a smooth, trouble-free relationship, you must have an operating agreement that works for both parties.

Reverse Logistics Contracts

Crafting a 3PL contract for returns management is significantly different, in a number of ways, from a traditional supply chain service agreement. The biggest reason for this is that, with returns, nobody knows for certain what you are going to receive, when you are going to receive it, or what condition it will be in when it arrives. You don't order returns from a supplier. Flexibility is critical.

In the world of reverse logistics, there are two types of contracts. The first type is a variable-rate contract and the second type is bad. Fixed-rate contracts for reverse logistics are never good for either the service provider or the customer. Somebody is going to lose sooner or later; and the argument that ensues will be bitter.

Variable-rate contracts are the only types of contract that will provide a win-win opportunity for both the customer and the 3PL. Variable rate means some form of cost, plus a management fee contract. The vast majority of contracts governing return center operations are, in fact, some form of cost -plus. This can come in a number of tailored formats but for the most part, the 3PL is paid their full cost of operation plus a management fee. Generally, there is a budgetary cap but the agreement is cost-plus based on a predetermined set of assumptions and volume of products to be returned or processed. While fees may vary based on the services provided, costs are supposed to be what the 3PL actually paid to provide the service. Here is where many companies **overpay**. For most, this overpayment can be avoided by asking a few questions upfront and closely reviewing invoices throughout the life of the contract.

As stated earlier, cost-plus contracts are designed to charge the customer for the actual cost paid for all goods and services used to deliver the service, plus a management fee, which, in theory, is the profit margin for the 3PL.

3PL Contract Language Tips

How you craft the agreement is critical to whether the agreement is truly a win-win or win-lose contract. There are four areas that companies should consider when negotiating an agreement with the 3PL and when paying the 3PLs invoices.

The first area of focus is employee benefits. Unless specified in the contract, benefits charged on wages should be the actual cost of the benefits. That means that rebates that the 3PL gets on health insurance and worker's compensation should be credited to the customer. If operating under a cost-plus contract, a customer is charged a "standard percentage" by the 3PL---no rebate is ever passed on as a future invoice credit--- the customer is being overcharged.

This is an all-too-common occurrence for worker's compensation expenses, health insurance expenses, and temp agency costs over an extended period of time. Unfortunately, for the uninitiated, these categories are generally not clearly addressed in contracts. Neither party raises it as an issue other than to present or pay the bill.

If, however, the contract stipulates that there is to be a standard percentage applied to wages for these categories, then the charge is simply the percentage applied to actual wages. Depending on the benefits impacted and the demographics of the workforce, this can work for, or against, the customer or 3PL. Remember, in many operations, hourly wages can be as much as forty to fifty-five percent of total operations costs. (12) Benefits on those wages can be as much as thirty-five percent of labor expenses. (12) impacts this large requires laser focus on how these costs are addressed in the contract and how the charges will be invoiced. Being charged a few extra points over cost-of-benefits by ignoring the rebate, results in significant money over the life of the contract.

The next area to consider is temporary labor charges. Many temp agencies offer rebates to 3PLs based on volume over a three-month period or longer; it can be up to a year. Customers have the right to see these service agreements, and all side letters that determine their billings. Customers can, and should, call the temp agency to discuss the specific arrangements. If there is a rebate from a temp agency, or from any supplier for that matter, based on volume purchases, customers should receive their fair share of the rebate. This is assuming that the contract is built on a cost-plus basis and that the specific rebates were not mentioned directly. Cost-plus or fixed, the signed contract is the last word on each party's rights and obligations.

Next, many operators also provide systems and systems support. While support typically is based on a percentage of the software license fee, the actual systems license costs are much less and, in reality, are in large part, profit. You will hear arguments that the license costs have to cover a lot of research and development (R&D), overhead, and other indirect costs that the customer never sees. The truth is that the vast majority of license fees and maintenance billings are pure profit. Primarily, because of this fact, it is a standard industry practice not to charge a management fee on software-related costs. This is one of the areas that should be addressed up front in contract negotiations. If it isn't spelled out or included as a budget line item, you should not be charged a management fee.

The last point to carefully examine is corporate allocation of charges for overhead commonly known as sales general and administration. (SG&A) Like the areas noted above, unless this amount is clearly defined as a percentage of total costs or something similar, it should be the actual costs. The big mistake that many buyers of 3PL services make, however, is that they pay a management fee on top of a corporate allocation and overhead. In effect, compounding the fee paid to the provider.

Most experienced supply chain executives exclude charges associated with corporate allocation of overhead from the start. There should only be one fee to negotiate. Don't allow yourself to be put in the position of negotiating two, three, or four fees depending on the activity. This is a tactic used by some 3PLs to simply confuse the issue and ultimately, make more profit.

Third-party logistics experience pays when it comes to nego-tiating 3PL agreements, especially ones made on a cost-plus basis. Taking a few courses in contract negotiation or having the title of vice president of procurement does not qualify an executive to craft the most advantageous 3PL agreement. Real-world experience is needed to uncover hidden contract landmines and ensure a thorough under-standing of every aspect of it. Some executives foolishly underesti-mate the complexities of returns processing. Just because it is returns does not mean it isn't very complicated.

Cost-Plus Contracts

The most important part of a cost-plus contract is the attachments that address variable budgets that are based on the assumed volume. This budget provides four important components that both parties will rely upon in the future.

First, the budget should have a list of assumptions that were used to calculate the amounts. These assumptions should be used as a basis for calculating future invoices and the actual "volume adjusted bud-get" that will be used to determine if the 3PL is successful in meeting budget-cost commitments. Assumptions usually include items such as assumed volume, burden rates, lease costs, maintenance factors, full-time equivalent hours worked in a year, software costs, deprecia-tion factors, and many more line-item calculations.

This budget also serves as a format for calculations that will be used to bill for services rendered. Customers using 3PLs should in-sist that invoices and supporting documentation follow the format and structure of the budget attached to the contract. This is a best-practice that can make managing a 3PL contract much easier on a month in month out basis.

Variable cost budgets should clearly differentiate variable-expense line items, which are, subject to volume adjustments, and line items that are fixed expenses. In addition, line items used to cal-culate management fees should be clearly identified. Finally, determine which line items are not subject to fees. With this information, a volume-adjusted budget can be accurately calculated.

An easy way to decide what should be a fixed line item and what should be variable is to ask if a given expense will increase and decrease with volume. Loading dockworkers' salaries are a variable expense, but the janitor's or the facility manager's salary is a fixed expense.

Variable and fixed-cost designations determine how the volume-adjusted budget is calculated. Fixed expenses are, what they are. The dollars don't change month to month, for the most part. Variable expenses are broken down as a cost-per-unit. The cost-per-unit is then applied to the volume, which determines the total volume-adjusted, variable budget amount. This amount is added to the fixed expense total, fees, and "below the line" items. Voilà! An accurate, volume-adjusted budget to compare to the actual expenses incurred is born.

There are many areas of caution companies must recognize when negotiating and managing 3PL agreements. Likewise, there are just as many areas of concern for the 3PL. The key to a long lasting, win-win relationship is to document as many assumptions and expectations as possible; identify all the variable and fixed expenses; and incorporate flexibility and reviewability throughout the life of the agreement.

Monitoring A 3PL

The review process is often overlooked but is critical to both customer and service provider. The administration of the contract must be done in a spirit of cooperation and understanding. It will be a short-term, unsatisfying agreement if common sense and fairness are not uniformly applied. That is not to say that one party must underwrite the other party's failures; but it does mean that each party should listen and react to the other's legitimate concerns.

Outsourced supply chain functions should not, and does not, run on autopilot. There are too many variables and market dynamics that impact both sides to justify unattended business functions, outsourced or not. Incorporating a quarterly review process in the agreement is one way to make sure a collaborative review of results and upcoming issues will take place on a regular basis.

During the start-up phase of an operation, the parties may want to meet monthly or weekly. These meeting should be face-to-face over a carefully considered, pre-published agenda. In addition to these meetings, it wouldn't be unusual to have a daily or weekly conference call where both parties review a project, productivity, and/or a ramp-up plan. In the beginning of any relationship it is impossible to over communicate.

Once the facility is up and running, quarterly meetings will suffice. These meetings will not replace regular communications on detailed, daily activities. Quarterly meetings are a forum for review of the previous three months' activities and a discussion of the plans for the next three months. Senior leadership from both parties should be in attendance at quarterly meetings.

This high-level involvement is critical to ensure good communication and foster free-flowing discussion of opportunities for both parties to improve joint and internal operations. This type of an open forum creates an atmosphere of trust and cooperation in which issues can be resolved and conflict avoided. Having senior management engaged can also yield surprising results. As a 3pl representative, I have been in a number of quarterly meetings where the onsite manager of the customer was pushing back on an issue only to have his boss's boss side with us and end the conflict.

The quarterly meetings really serve two purposes. First they review the concrete performance and plans of the operation. This is important to ensure everyone is on the same page. Reviewing the numbers and plans also allows both teams to work together to improve forecasting and planning and solve problems for their mutual benefit.

More importantly, however, the quarterly meetings set expectations and measure performance against those expectations. This is why it is vital that the senior leadership from both sides attend these meetings. You cannot trust your manager to communicate everything correctly. You cannot trust your customer's onsite manager to accurately communicate every operational detail. Having the senior decision makers in the room from both sides ensures that the message delivered and the response given is accurate.

From a service provider's point of view, exposure to your customer's senior leadership is incredibly valuable. It is at this level that a successful relationship is formed to nurture the account and bring it to maturity. Building relationships at this level is also the best way to prevent your operation from being the subject of an RFP at the end of the contract. Additionally, these meetings provide an environment to mine additional business that will address the customer's needs.

When I was responsible for sales and marketing at a large 3PL in North America, I tracked close-rates for new business versus new sales to existing customers. The close rate for new sales to existing customers was twice that of prospect proposals. I have since found that this metric is true for every business but only if the senior leadership team is directly involved in building relationships with their customer counterparts. (8)

Customers also want to have a strong relationship with the top decision-makers of their service providers. They want to know the person that they call in the middle of the night. Once a customer builds a trusted relationship with a top decision maker, that trust will often lead to new business.

CHAPTER 6

Product Recalls

In the world of reverse logistics, there are two major categories of returned assets. The one most often thought of is normal, defective or customer returns. These are products that have been purchased and returned by the customer for any number of reasons. The second major category of reverse logistics pipeline assets is referred to as product recalls.

Recalls are products that may or may not have been sold to the end user and are being withdrawn from their primary channel of commerce. Products are recalled because they are obsolete, out of season, simply not selling, or pose a threat to the public, to name a few reasons. Recalls are also referred to as guaranteed sale returns, merchandise returns, stock pulls, seasonal pulls, or stock outs. Regardless of what they are called, the purpose and the process is the same. Recalls are simply products that did sell or cannot be sold and are being taken off the market.

In the mid 1990s when I was responsible for Sears' return center operations, I received a call from our senior point of contact at Sears notifying us of a major seasonal recall that had just been ordered by the CEO of Sears. This took place during the prime Christmas selling season and it was critical that the product be immediately recalled. This was a top priority coming directly from the CEO's office.

This was not a typical recall. As it turned out, the product recalled was Christmas tree bells. It seemed kind of odd but I thought it was a recall due to some factory flaw or potential liability. When the Christmas bells arrived in the return center, it became clear that some recalls are made just because the CEO orders them.

This particular set of Christmas bells depicted famous cartoon characters that were linked together in long strings. Between each character was a bell. When the strand of bells was plugged in, the cartoon characters, which were about three inches tall, would pivot left and right, striking the bells with their "dingers".

This is where the problem started. The "dingers" were half inch long golden rods with a knob on the end. The knob struck the bell as the characters pivoted back and forth with big smiles on their cute little faces. To add a touch of realism, I suppose, the cartoon characters were fashioned with both hands firmly gasping their golden "dingers," waste high.

According the manager of reverse logistics at Sears, a lady, who had been doing her Christmas shopping, was offended by the cartoon characters she saw on display. She, called the CEO of Sears enraged that they were selling Christmas bells with cartoon characters holding there, well, let's just refer to them as "dingers". The CEO was so embarrassed when he saw the actual product that he ordered all the product off the shelves. What's more, the CEO requested certification of destruction to ensure they did not "pop up" anywhere else. This is an example of one of the possible reasons for a recall.(8)

Often, products are recalled due to problems with packaging. In the 1990s when homemade bread makers first hit the market, the initial customer return rate for one of the more popular brands was over fifty percent. The manufacturer's team descended on a centralized return facility that was processing the item to inspect the returned bread makers to determine why the return rate was so high.

After about three days of testing, the vast majority of bread makers were found to work perfectly. Based on the test results of the product at the return center, the actual defective rate was less than ten percent. The question was "Why were so many of these bread makers returned, if there was nothing functionally wrong with the appliance itself?"

The instruction manual, the power supplies, the packaging---all were thoroughly reviewed and checked. Even a new unit was purchased and bread was baked, right in the return center! That was when the team figured out the problem.

The reason for the high return rate was not because of the appliance at all. The problem was that on the outside of the packaging, there was nice-looking, long, rectangular loaf of bread. The loaf of bread that came out of the homemade bread maker was actually round. The bread tasted great but it didn't look anything like the picture on the outside of the box! Customers who purchased the bread maker thought it was defective because the loaf of bread didn't look anything like the picture.

As a result, the company ordered an immediate recall on the bread makers. When the product was received back into the returns facilities, a new label was slapped on the side of every unit with a picture of a nice round loaf of bread on a plate next to the bread maker. The re-labeled bread makers were immediately shipped back to the retailers and were a favorite during the Christmas season. The post-recall return rate was under ten percent of sales, just as the manufacturer and retailer had planned.

This is another example of why products are recalled but more importantly, it shows that companies can leverage recall capabilities to correct many issues, thus reducing costs and increasing sales and profits.

Major Causes of Recalls

Bad buying decisions are one of the primary reasons for recalls. Every year, merchandise buyers around the globe buy too much of one or more items; resulting in recalling and replacing them with items of higher demand or more profitability.

Most perfume and fragrance manufactures recall gifts sets every year after Christmas and Mothers Day. These gift sets are broken down and the individual pieces are repackaged for sale in the primary channel as individual items. Reprocessing costs for perfumes and fragrances are typically less than ten percent of the cost of manufacturing a new item. Because of this, their manufacturers use the recall process as a key strategy for sourcing product and maximizing sales throughout the year.

Perhaps the most well-known reason for recalling items is government-ordered removal from the marketplace. Every year for the past twenty years, for example, the U.S. Food and Drug Administration (FDA) has ordered between two and three hundred pharmaceutical products be taken out of the stream of commerce. Most of these recalls have gone unnoticed because the products were recalled for reasons other than any adverse effects they may have on people who have taken the drug.

Many widely-publicized pharmaceutical recalls for serious adverse effects such as death, or other health problems, the truth is the vast majority of pharmaceutical recalls are for reasons such as a microscopic variance in the chemical compound; or some quality issue with packaging; or an issue with the labels and inserts. The pharmaceutical companies regularly recall drugs for a variety of reasons, most of which don't pose a threat to public welfare.

Pharmaceutical Recalls

In the world of pharmaceutical recalls, there are three different levels. These levels are established based on where the recalled product is located; which is determined by the severity of the danger posed by the drug to the public.

The first level of pharmaceutical recalls is from the distributor or wholesale level, which is commonly known as a Class III recall. In a Class III recall, any and all product located in a warehouse or distribution center is pulled from the shelves and returned to the manufacturer. This level does not pertain to product located at a doctor's office, hospital, retail store, or patient's home. Drugs in these locations are dispensed in the ordinary course of business until they are completely consumed.

The second level or Class II, pharmaceutical recall occurs when product must be removed from the distributor or wholesale level, retail stores, hospitals, and doctors' offices. A Class II recall removes all the drugs from the market except those in the possession of the consumer.

The third level of pharmaceutical recalls, referred to as "Class I" recalls, is when all of the product is recalled from the supply chain including that, which is in the possession of the consumer. Pharmaceutical companies are required by law to take extensive measures to notify not only the companies that purchased the drugs from them, but also all of the patients who have received prescriptions for the recalled medication. Often, pharmaceutical manufacturers mail flyers, and in some instances produce television commercials, informing the public of the recall and instructing them what to do with any product that they may have. These are the recalls that make the news and may ultimately involve expensive litigation. Thanks to the FDA, as well as careful testing and high-quality manufacturing throughout the pharmaceutical industry, this level of recall is very rare.

There are other government regulatory agencies which govern and oversee the manufacturing of products; these agencies often initiate and monitor product recalls. Often these recalls are ordered as a result of a significant number of accidents, or injuries caused by a design flaw in a product. These types of recalls have included products such as infant cribs and other baby products, cars parts, desk lamps, and computer batteries. Any item that poses a threat to public health and safety can, and has been recalled.

Because of the potential liability and responsibility to the public, retailers, distributers and manufacturers should have a recall plan and processes established to ensure a timely reaction to any type of product recall. Whether voluntary or mandatory, recalls are fraught with potential liability and risk to human life, making a well-thought-out plan essential. If a company waits until a recall is ordered, the cost and the additional liability might, literally, put them out of business. Lawsuits, fines, logistics, and cleanup costs are real consequences of a product recall.

Sometimes, product recalls create exposure to unanticipated risks or consequences. These risks include: negative employee moral resulting from actions taken by the company during a recall; shareholder concerns or lawsuits; and customer attitudes which are affected by negative or positive press on the recall.

A Comprehensive Recall Procedure

Developing a recall procedure (whether parts of the process are outsourced or not) is clearly critical to every company that makes or sells product. There are five key components that must be considered when developing or evaluating a recall procedure. They are:

- Internal communications procedure
- External communications procedure
- Physical process of removing the recalled products from the supply chain
- Product sorting, accounting, and disposal process
- Data-gathering, reporting, and record keeping

Let us discuss each component of a well-developed recall procedure. As you will see, a recall procedure must be a well-coordinated, pre-defined process in order to achieve the ultimate goal of the recall procedure. The ultimate goal of a recall procedure is to provide a responsible, time-sensitive method to recall product from the supply chain while minimizing the overall cost and liability to the organization.

Internal communications in a situation where a company has either voluntarily or mandatorily initiated a recall that has "adverse effects" starts with an emergency internal communications chain. This is simply determining who is going to be notified, how they are going to be notified, and what their responsibility is in the recall process. Speed is critical. Any product that has been recalled, whether it is re-called because it is obsolete or it poses some danger to the public, will not get better with time. In fact, time is your enemy in a recall situation. The longer a company waits to act, the risk of liability and recall costs increase.

The line of internal communication must be clear and deliberate. The first hours after being notified of a recall will determine whether or not the remainder of the recall plan can succeed. The internal communications process is the starting pistol in the race to get the recalled products off the market and out of the supply chain. A critical element of the internal communications plan is to clearly designate who is going to speak publicly on behalf of the company, what they are going to say, and whom they are going to say it to. Despite temp-tations to do otherwise, it is always better to be completely open and honest with everyone, especially regulators.

Deciding what to say and when to say it is more about who is going to receive the message, when they will be told, and who inside the organization is going to deliver the message. It isn't about twisting the truth or trying to spin a story. Companies that twist and distort the truth pay a heavy price both in monetary terms and also in terms of the long-term reputation of the company with customers, employees, and other stakeholders. If you have any doubt, remember the impact of the recent high-profile automotive company recalls. The press was brutal. Press coverage had an enormous impact on public perception of the automotive company in question and sub-sequently, an enormous negative impact on sales.

External communications is probably the most critical compo-nent to minimizing the impact of a recall on customers, employees, and shareholders. Again, honesty is the best policy. It is actually the only policy that works. You must be prepared to communicate openly and honestly.

In the case of major or high profile recalls employees will want to hear directly from the CEO. They will want, and need, regular updates. They will want, and deserve, closure when the recall is completed. Remember, employees have families and friends who will ask them about the recall. You must arm employees with the enough information about what the company is doing to reduce any threat or danger so they can communicate accurately and completely with their constituents. (family, friends, neighbors) Employees need to feel positively about their work and the company that employs them. Many organizations underestimate the impact of bad press or no information on employees. Consistent, open communication with employees not only strengthens internal relationships but can also strengthen a company's financial position when a recall is in progress by building good will and customer loyalty. This good will starts with your employees who serve as ambassadors in the community-at-large. It is a very important to them and can cost a company more than just money if not addressed properly. Keep in mind that for many organizations, employees are the only spokesmen in the local communities most of their customers can talk to about an issue.

Shareholders will have similar concerns and they have a legal right to know about potential liabilities that could have a negative impact on their investment. There have been a number of companies that have never recovered after management botched external communications. Once the investment community and the public loses faith and trust in the management team, investors will move their money to more reliable investments and customers will shop elsewhere.

An important part of any external communications strategy is determining how best to deal with the press. Talking to the press can be very tricky anytime, but especially when addressing product recalls, which almost universally treated as negative news.

I have personally been involved in 8 to 10 stories that were reported on in the press and I am sad to report that the media did not get the story correct even one time. (12)

It is important to remember that journalists are there to get a story that will sell papers or improve ratings. Getting the story right or being fair to all the involved parties is not a high priority. Reporters move fast and most invest little time trying to understand all the facts. They look for attention grabbing headlines and will be more than happy to risk ruining reputations in the process of writing a sensational story. Not all reporters are this way, but enough are that you should be wary and purposeful in your communications. This is why a public relations professional can be worth their weight in gold during a major recall.

A major recall is not the time for an inexperienced executive to try his hand at dealing with the press. A great rule of thumb is simply to tell everyone to always respond politely, "No comment." If a company wants or needs to disseminate information to the public about the recall, hire a professional. The public has a right to know about things that might impact them and it is in a company's best interest to be forthcoming and informative so that the impact of rumors and misinformation is minimized.

The last group to address in your external communications plan is the regulators. There are two ways management teams can deal with regulators. One way is to treat them as adversaries. Don't offer any help. Answer only the exact question asked. Make them get a court order for everything. This approach is a sure-fire way to draw a lot more attention from the regulators; clearly not advisable.

The other regulator approach is to cooperate fully. This means to be polite. Escort them around your facility. Ask them if they need help with anything. Politely say things like, "Sir, I was told to buy you a cup of coffee and set you up in my office until our vice president of loss prevention arrives. This situation is important to us and we want to cooperate fully. We want our best and brightest here to assist you with your needs so please bear with us for a few minutes until everyone arrives." Then, go get the coffee.

While regulators should always be treated politely and companies should fully cooperate with them in their investigation, a certain amount of common sense should apply. A core executive team should take the lead on all interactions with the regulators. The executive team should focus on communicating with regulators and clearly conveying corporate expectations to employees who interact with the regulators. Just as in dealing with the press, bring in the professionals. Every company should have experienced legal counsel they can call on in times of need. While this may seem initially expensive, the long-term repercussions of mishandling regulators can result in significantly greater fines and penalties, including jail time in some cases.

While involving legal counsel and having an executive communications team is highly recommended, being cooperative is the only way to deal with any kind of recall regulator. You must ensure that your entire staff is trained to be polite and cooperative. They must have a clear idea of what they should and should not say. They must know the difference between being cooperative and saying things that are simply speculation on their part. Facts are what are required, not conjecture.

The next component of a recall process is removing the product from the marketplace. There are three steps to removing the product. First, companies must have a way to communicate to the parties that are currently in possession of the recalled goods. If product is only being pulled from the wholesale and distribution network, simply calling and emailing key management may suffice. If a manufacturer is recalling from the retail level, they may only have to notify point people in the retailer's organization. Almost all retailers have a well-developed communications process for store-level recalls. This greatly simplifies the recall process for their manufacturers.

In some cases, however, companies may have to notify the public. This can be done through direct mail, newspaper advertisements, television announcements, and press releases. It is important for companies to make every effort to inform all of the impacted parties.

Notifying the holders of the recalled product should include clear handling and shipping instructions. For pharmaceutical recalls, a Form 222 is used to request that the recipient send back part of the form with the returned quantities of the recalled items listed on the form. This form is used by the FDA to determine the efficacy of the recall notification process. It can also be used to receive the product when it is shipped to their recall processing center.

A small parcel carrier is generally used for recalls of products that might be hazardous to the public, has a high value, or poses some other significant threat. Many times, recalled consumer goods are simply returned to the store-of-purchase from which it is shipped to the recall processor or a return center via less-than-truckload (LTL) or truckload carrier.

Once the product is received at the facility where the recall is being processed, quantities and other pertinent information, such as lot number, are documented. The product is then sorted by SKU and held until the regulatory authority gives permission to ship the product to its final destination for disposal or destruction. When receiving the product, the recall processor should record receipt, quantity and condition by sender. If tracking codes, batch numbers, or lot codes were used to recall the goods this information should be captured as well.

No packaging, paperwork, or product should be altered, tampered with or destroyed without a regulator's approval. (if a regulator is involved) That is to say, if a regulator has been involved with the process, don't take any steps without their approval. After product is comingled, questions about condition and where a particular product came from cannot easily be answered. A company's ability to provide this information and answer these questions can reduce their liability and avoid additional processing costs or fines.

The last critical component in a recall process is data gathering, storage and reporting. There are legions of lawyers that eagerly await news of a recall. They look for opportunities to pounce and many times, companies are actually victims of their own lack of record keeping. Collecting data and having the ability to develop reports related to a recall can save a company, literally, millions in legal fees, penalties, and bad press.

Recall Reporting

When developing recall-reporting protocols, there are three distinct junctures in the process where a company should capture data and provide reporting. They are:

- Product receipt – who sent the product to the recall facility, and all associated information
- Recall Processing – what individual items, or SKUs were processed, how were they processed, along with detailed inventory reports tracking inbound receipts through to shipping
- Disposition – what were the various ways the recalled product was disposed of, i.e., incineration, landfill, repaired, recycled, etc. Disposition by item, SKU, batch, or lot may be required depending on the item recalled and the regulatory agency overseeing the recall

A wise practice is to mandate that both the recall processor to whom the task is outsourced and the company keeps a copy of the recall source documents, processing data, and final disposition reports for at least seven years. In every situation, however, always consult with qualified legal counsel to ensure that all involved parties are proceeding prudently and according to legal statute to minimize risks associated with product recalls.

CHAPTER 7

Salvage, Liquidation, and Asset Recovery

Perhaps the biggest surprise to executives new to the reverse logistics industry is the value and potential of liquidation. For most consumer product manufacturers and virtually all non-food retailers, roughly one-half of all returns are eventually sold on the secondary market.

The secondary market is comprised of many different types of re-sellers. Value retailers, flea markets, mom-and-pop online auction sellers, and large salvage brokers are the varied business models that make up the secondary market. From the small operator who sets up a table at your local flea market to large publicly traded companies the secondary market is a diverse and integral part of reverse logistics.

Remember, the study conducted by Dr. Dale Rogers that determined that the secondary retail market comprises 2.28% of U.S. GDP? (4) (Rogers) This percentage is roughly the size of Walmart and, in total, more profitable. The chart below illustrates the sectors of the secondary market in the United States and the percentage of revenue by class. Pawnshops and charities also comprise part of the secondary market but their share of the pie is less than one percent of the total and is not shown in this chart.

Dr. James Stock's study further strengthens the illustration when he discovered that, in 2009, U.S. consumers returned product with a higher dollar value than the GDP of sixty-six nations of the world! (page 34)

Annual Secondary Market Sales Is 2.28% of US GDP

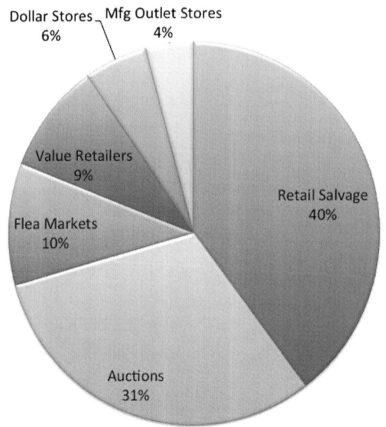

Dollar Stores 6% — Mfg Outlet Stores 4%
Value Retailers 9%
Flea Markets 10%
Retail Salvage 40%
Auctions 31%

Based on our experience, of the $194 billion in 2010 consumer returns (5), approximately fifty percent were ultimately sold on the secondary market. (8) There is a profit-generating, secondary market for virtually everything, regardless of condition, in the reverse logistics marketplace and it is the largest profit generator in the reverse logistics market.

The Secondary Market is Recession Proof

When the economy turns; the secondary market explodes. However, you must know the market and understand how it works. There are many different players who all seem to know each other. Also, it is the ultimate supply and demand market.

The value of product liquidated dramatically increases and decreases for reasons that have nothing to do with the parties involved or the product being bought or sold.

A few years ago I was involved with a deal to liquidate a very popular MP3 player. We bid to buy the players from a well-known retailer who could not return the MP3 players for credit.

We bid a very aggressive fifty-five percent of current retail; and won the bid. We took possession of the goods the following week and began to refurbish them for online re-sale for seventy percent of regular retail over the next thirty days. That was our plan. However, you know what they say about the best-laid plans.

Within one week of buying and taking possession of the MP3 players, the same manufacturer of our MP3 players introduced an upgraded product that had video capabilities and was one half the price of the older models we had bought. Over the course of a week, a great buy turned into a money loser. So goes the secondary market.(8)

Liquidation, also known as Asset Recovery, is not a business for the fainthearted. Liquidation takes commitment. You must be prepared to lose money now and then on a few deals in order to make a lot of money over the long haul. Liquidation is dynamic and takes a well-developed process, overseen by professionals, to ensure profitability. If the right processes and people are in place, companies can make a substantial profit.

If you examined the average retailer's inventory, you would find that roughly six percent of total purchases are returned by consumers within thirty days of purchase. During my twenty-five-plus years in the business, I can tell you that more than one half of all returns are not defective at all. They are returned for some excuse that is typically a variation of buyer's remorse. (8)

Most retailers return approximately one half of all returns to the manufacturer and sell the remainder on the secondary market. (8) Some refer to this product as salvage, some call it liquidation, some call it asset recovery, but **they all call it profitable.** Selling product on the secondary market is like alchemy but instead of lead to gold, it turns trash into cash.

What many don't realize is that there is a great deal of product that has never been sold to a consumer that is ultimately sold on the secondary market. This inventory comes from seasonal product that didn't sell by the end of the season, over-buys that can't be returned to the seller, and product that is recalled by the manufacturer or the retailer. If you shop at a Marshalls, T.J. Maxx, or Big Lots Odd Lots you know all about this kind of product.

How Buyers Bid on Salvage Loads

Regardless of why the product is relegated to the secondary market, there is a formula that salvage buyers use to calculate what they will pay for the product. That formula works like this:

(Retail x 75% x % Yield) / 2 – Transportation = Salvage Buyer Bid

There are some important variables involved, but for the most part, salvage buyers work on a fifty percent margin, assuming a certain amount (% Yield) of product that can be sold for roughly 75% of the cost of a brand new item. From that, they subtract transportation, which is usually paid for by the salvage buyer, which leaves the amount the salvage buyer will pay for the returned or recalled product.

However, this is the land of supply and demand. Depending on the supply and demand situation, bids will fluctuate significantly. Other factors also impact demand and, therefore, the price paid on the secondary market. A good example product of this is the Apple iPod. A year ago, refurbished iPods were being sold on the secondary market for $100. (cite source) Then, Apple dropped the price of new iPods to $100 and the inventory that was in high demand at $100 had to be sold at a significantly lower price. (8)

The secondary market is not for rookies. There is a wide network of very smart, experienced people who buy and sell product just like Wall Street traders buy and sell stocks. If you want to jump in the market, hire a liquidation expert, or become one but don't underestimate a liquidation professional.

Whether you are looking to get into the liquidation business or if you are thinking of turning your trash into cash, now you have an idea of how the secondary market works. Here's to bigger profits and turning trash to cash! The following diagram provides an overview of the secondary market and how product flows from retailers and OEMs to the ultimate customer who buys the product on the secondary market.

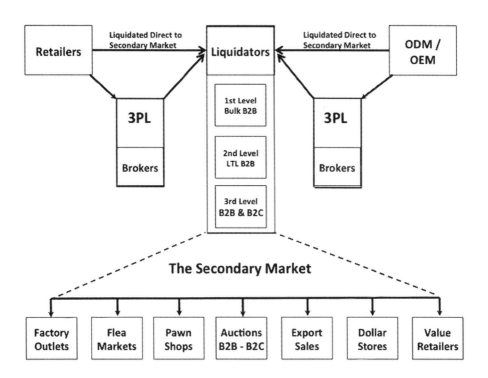

CHAPTER 8

Managing Transportation Expenses

Managing returns is a business function that most companies prefer to ignore. Unfortunately, dealing with returns is a fact of life for every retailer. To effectively manage a reverse logistics supply chain, you must understand that there are a number of important support areas that have a significant impact on the cost of processing assets that flow through the reverse logistics pipeline.

One of the most high-impact support areas is the transportation department. Over the next ten years, transportation expenses will increase more quickly and impact reverse logistics more extensively than any other support function in the reverse logistics ecosystem. Factors such as rising fuel prices, truck driver shortages, and increased regulation will force transportation executives to rethink their reverse logistics network in light of the new cost reality.

In fact, transportation costs will be the primary, motivating factor behind the strategic network redesign of virtually every reverse logistics supply chain. To mitigate the financial impact, there are a number of best practices companies can establish and employ. Realized savings will only grow with time, as will the importance of understanding and using the thought process behind these best practices.

The recommendations and approaches included in this chapter are the result of working with many companies around the world for more than twenty-five years and helping them improve their reverse logistics processes. These best practices address errors in design that companies initially made at the onset of processing returns.

The time to develop a returns handling process---devoting resources to returns management---is BEFORE a company begins to receive returns in a critical mass. In the early stages of returns-processing development, companies typically look to the vice president of transportation formulate a process that moves returned assets from point A to point B.

Transportation executives, who are largely unfamiliar with reverse logistics processes, would naturally turn to models applied to managing forward transportation of goods. They might think that, compared to the volume of goods and the complexity of managing transportation for new goods, developing unique cost models for the transportation of used goods is not worth the extra time and effort. Thus, the existing infrastructure, processes, and costing systems that are used for outbound transportation are foolishly used for returned goods. Therein, lies the problem.

Transportation, in the world of reverse logistics, must be designed with unique, different terms and conditions (Ts & Cs) than typical forward transportation. Just as driving your car in reverse requires a different approach and posture than driving your vehicle forward, transportation agreements that govern moving goods through a reverse pipeline require different terms, conditions, and controls to properly manage transportation and its related costs.

Managing transportation costs is one of those often-overlooked areas when designing reverse logistics processes. Very often, the internal traffic department is completely excluded from the discussion or folded into it at the back end. Excluding transportation as an integral piece in developing reverse logistics solutions always results in higher costs.

While moving products in reverse, the control mechanisms that exist in the forward supply chain either don't exist or are in the wrong location within the supply chain infrastructure. For example, a retail company may have great LTL rates for goods shipped from their distribution centers to their stores. The pallets are weighed and put on the appropriate trailer along with the manifest and other shipping documents that have been efficiently produced by the transportation system or warehouse management system. When the truck arrives at the back of the store, the receiving manager simply signs for load and verifies that everything on the manifest is received. Now, let's reverse this.

The store moves all the returned, defective, and recalled goods from the customer service desk to the stock room. Here, it is recorded and prepared to return to the company's return or distribution center. If you used the same transportation processes and controls as the forward process, the store would first have to weigh the shipment before it is loaded onto a truck.

STOP!! This is where the problems start. Stores usually do not have a scale in the back of the store to weigh a pallet. For those executives who don't work with transportation terms, traditional carrier contracts are based on a cost-per-one -hundred pounds shipped, commonly referred to as cost per hundred-weight (CWT). CWT is the unit of measure for charging and transporting products. This is the common basis for carrier contracts used since the 1800s. Using this standard, the trucking company charges its customers a negotiated dollar amount for every one hundred pounds of product shipped. In returns processing, calculating transportation costs in this way poses a significant problem. Assume for a second that you actually do have a scale at store-level to weigh the pallet. Once weighed, a proper shipping manifest that lists all the items in the shipment must be produced. Again, these manifesting systems typically only reside in the distribution center, not in the store.

Assuming the same systems, processes, and agreements that are used going forward is not a best practice in reverse. In fact, it is not even practical. Not only will this not work efficiently, it will cost a lot more money. Using a traditional transportation processes to move assets through the reverse logistics pipeline results either in losing control, inflating transportation costs or both.

Most often, manufacturers and retailers ship customer returns and recalled product in LTL quantities. The standards and methods employed in moving product forward are often built into the process when the carrier contracts are negotiated, thus ensuring poor controls and inflated costs.

While the aforementioned CWT standard for forward distribution of product does not work for transporting returns. As previously mentioned, the problem is that the vast majority of reverse logistics networks do not have a way to verify the weight of a pallet of returns at the point where the pallet is created. When this happens, the company shipping the returns must rely on the weight reported by the carrier to determine how much is to be paid for transporting the load of returns. This lack of verification and control can lead to many problems, the largest of which is paying too much in freight charges. In addition, products are generally not returned in nice new cartons or in over-wraps that will hold up well during shipping.

Standard methods used to identify inventory and to file freight claims are also compromised. Odd-sized items such as ladders, power tools, and knockdown furniture are problematic. To top it all off, literally, in an effort to maximize a trailer's cube utilization, carriers will often double-stack pallets of returns, which causes a significant amount of damage and loss of recovery value.

Transporting returned goods that are later re-classified as hazardous materials can be complicated and very costly. The largest lawsuit ever brought against a business by the State of California was one involving the transportation of returned goods from a retailer's stores to its return center. The products shipped were widely used consumer goods that the majority of the world uses every day---nuclear waste. The State of California took exception to the retailer using the long-standing practice of shipping returns to their return center as non-hazardous product. At the returns facility, the products were reclassified as hazardous and processed for appropriate destruction. The State of California said no! The State ruled that products such as shampoo and household cleaners were, in fact, "hazardous." The requirements for shipping returns classified as hazardous material are much more complicated. The liability is exponentially larger. The cost of transportation is three to four times higher than non-hazardous shipping charges.

Because of the complexities of moving hazardous goods out of the primary stream of commerce, manufacturers of particularly dangerous products utilize special reverse logistics transportation services. Manufacturers of car batteries, pool chemicals, and pesticides have well-developed transportation procedures that should be followed. Transporting hazardous products using homegrown processes and systems is not worth the risk.

Let's set aside the issues related to moving hazardous material through the returns process. The majority of goods that move through the reverse logistics pipeline are normal, everyday, non-hazardous products. It is the development and use of appropriate agreements and efficient processes that makes reverse logistics profitable. The opportunity to save money is in establishing the right kind of agreements and processes to handle these goods.

In general, the best transportation contract for palletized returned goods is often not based on CWT but on the space the pallet of goods takes up on the trailer. Instead of negotiating a cost based on weight, write a contract based on the cost of space for one pallet on the trailer. Buying space on the trailer will actually discourage carriers from double stacking pallets, which can cause significant damage to returned goods that aren't packaged in their original cartons. Reducing the freight damage to returns will increase the assets recovery rate, which will fall directly to the bottom line. Carriers don't exactly love this method but they will eventually agree to this pricing method as long as they have the protection of a maximum weight per pallet, limited liability for claims which we will discuss later, and a piece rate for those odd shaped items referred to above.

You must be prepared to help convert CWT rates to a rate per pallet. It is simple and straightforward; but it is so foreign to carriers that they often need help calculating the rate. To calculate the rate per pallet, you will need the following:

- Average of pallets per trailer
- Average weight per pallet
- Average cube per pallet
- Carriers proposed CWT

Once you have these variables, work with the carrier to develop a cost per pallet. You will want to plan quarterly internal reviews of your assumptions and rate reviews with the carriers. These reviews will give both parties a way to mitigate any risks from any incorrect assumptions and changing variables. After a year or so, you may want to reduce the number of rate reviews to once, annually.

Transportation Based on Space

Setting up transportation based on space will give your employees who prepare the returns for shipment an opportunity to control transportation costs by insuring they "stack it high and tight". A key, measurable metric is quantity per pallet. An expected minimum should be established for the average quantity of product returned on a pallet. An example of palletizing instructions is: each pallet should hold an average of three hundred units, be at least six feet but no taller than eight feet high, and should not extend beyond the dimensions of the pallet itself. As the product is received or shipped, depending on the control points within your specific reverse pipeline, tracking the average units per pallet provides an easy way to minimize the cost-per-unit for transportation. Shipment inspections and feedback to the shippers will ensure proper pallet stacking and height.

Negotiating reverse logistics carrier rates based on space makes accounting and verification of the freight charges simple and straightforward. This method will eliminate the need for tare weight calculations and any debates on hub readings or other weight disputes.

Carrier Claims in the World of Returns

The last issue that must be addressed is carrier claims. Carrier claims for returned goods are a little more complex than normal claims because of difficulty in valuing the goods shipped. Traditional carrier claims are based on known items on a manifest, each with a market-driven value. In the world of reverse logistics, the shipper often does not exactly know what is in the "returned box" to begin with and the value could vary greatly depending on the terms, SKU, profile, condition, and age of the item. In addition multiple SKUs are often placed in a single carton. Neither the carrier nor the shipper have a reliable way to value freight claims because the relative value of the inventory can vary dramatically and there is a host of questions concerning how to price goods that may have missing components or are broken beyond repair.

The best, easiest, and most straightforward method with which to file freight claims is to establish an average value per case. This value is based on the budgeted units and total value of the products that are to be processed. The average value to per case should be included in the carrier contract and reviewed on an annual basis.

However, if the value of the product is significant, traditional freight claims valuation and processing should be used because the level of detail concerning the returned product is much greater using this method. In order to file traditional freight claims, an exact list of items shipped will need to be tracked for each shipment. If this level of detail is not possible, using an average value per case should be used.

Once you have established the average value per case that will be used for claims processing, procedures for stretch wrapping and securing pallet loads with security tape should be adopted. Each pallet should be stretch wrapped, capped with plastic or cardboard, and taped with unique security tape.

If the returned goods pallet is received and the stretch wrap and security tape are intact, the carrier is relieved of any liability for that pallet. If the stretch wrap or security tape appears to have been tampered with, the receiving facility should immediately count the number of cases on the pallet and compare the quantities to the signed manifest. If there is a shortage, or clear abusive damage, a claim should be filed using the average value per case.

Be Smart When Using Small Parcel Shipping

For many Internet retailers, pharmaceutical manufacturers, and high-value product sellers, small package contracts are used to return both defective and non-defective product from their customers. Using United Parcel Service (UPS), Federal Express (FedEx) United States Postal Service (USPS), Royal Post "or any other small package carrier makes a lot of sense on the outbound side. Many companies use these same services, with the same rates for returning the products.

Often, however, this is an area where companies can save a significant amount of money on transportation. Remember, when customers are returning product, all they are really concerned with is whether they get the right amount of credit in the next credit card billing cycle.

Customers aren't concerned with whether or not their return is processed within twenty-four hours. Many companies have great programs that enable customers to order products online and receive the product amazingly quickly. It is commonplace to have next-day delivery on almost everything,

But, why would you pay the premium small package fee to get returned product back the next day? Unless there is some product-driven reason, using the cheapest small package rate and shipping method won't impact anything other than company earnings. Many companies, however, by default, use the same rules for returns as they do for outbound shipments. Eliminating this practice reduces overpaying for unnecessary shipping and speed.

Some companies where they actually use overnight air to ship household appliances to the return center. To make matters worse, the return center had an average receiving backlog of three days. Companies that use this practice, pay a premium to get product back overnight, after which the unprocessed product sits on the dock for three days! When it comes to returns, intelligent speed, not raw speed, will always provide better customer service at a lower cost. Best-in-class organizations establish a customer-service-driven returns process that provides great customer service and minimizes the cost of transporting and processing assets in their reverse pipeline.

A Great Example of Customer Service and Returns

Recently, I had an excellent experience when I returned a Kindle I had purchased from Amazon.com. I had an entire library on my Kindle and I never left home without it. While on a business trip, I turned my Kindle on and the only thing that would come up on the screen was: "Your Kindle Needs Repair - Call Customer Service". As soon as I had the chance, I called customer service and received a pleasant surprise.

The customer service representative verified my identity and the serial number of my Kindle. Then said: "We are very sorry your Kindle is having this problem. We are going to overnight a replacement that will arrive at your house tomorrow between 2:00 and 5:00 p.m. When you receive the new Kindle, ship the old Kindle in the box the new one comes in, using the return UPS label. You can print the label on your computer using the link I will email you. Sir, you will have thirty days to return the defective Kindle. If we don't receive it in thirty days we will have to charge your credit card for the replacement. Do you have any questions?"

I was pleasantly surprised by the ease of Amazon' Kindle return process . I was thrilled that a replacement would arrive within twenty-four hours, and the returns process was so simple. Even I could do it. The next day, the new Kindle arrived, as promised. I had the email with the link that allowed me to easily print a completed UPS label, which I used to ship the item back to Amazon.com. While the new item received was shipped overnight via UPS, the outbound defective unit was not. The label that I printed used the slowest and cheapest UPS shipping method available. This is a great example of forward exchange/ returns program that was pleasant, efficient, customer centric, and cost effective. (8)

Many companies use similar forward exchange models that send the replacement to the customer immediately, receiving the defective part or unit days, or sometimes weeks later. Forward exchange programs are often used for critical parts, lease programs, and consumer goods warranty programs. Additionally, forward exchange is the norm when dealing with unique, high-value computer systems, medical devices, point-of-sale-systems, and Kindles. Forward exchange programs are to returns processing what Just in Time (JIT) programs are to forward distribution.

As with everything dealing with returns, the most important thing is to have a process that is easy on the customer. Studies have found that eighty-five percent of customers that had a bad returns experience say they will not make future purchases from the company. Conversely, ninety-five percent of customers who have a pleasant returns experience will buy again, whether they receive a refund or not. Companies such as Amazon.com, Walmart Stores, Target, Zappos, and Apple have realized huge dividends from developing a returns program that focuses on providing a positive customer experience.

I am sure that the cost of overnight shipping my new Kindle was built into the purchase price, but the Amazon.com experience seemed free and not having to pay anything at the time of the transaction made the entire experience a pleasant and positive one for me. (8)

A Best Practice for Return's Transportation Costs

The last best practice to help manage reverse logistics transportation expenses is successfully used by retailers, wholesalers, distributors, and manufacturers, but could easily work well for many business-to-business relationships. Because of the number of SKUs and the volume of products received, retailers generally have much better carrier contract pricing than do their manufacturing partners.

The best practice is to have retailers pay for the transportation returning the product to the manufacturer and to bill the manufacturers for the freight charges when processing the returns claims. This prepay-and-bill arrangement fits with most payable systems. However, when processing returns transportation there is a little twist that can save a lot of money for both parties. Generally, the cost of transportation is split between the retailer and the manufacturer. The retailer pays for the consolidation and the cost of transportation from their stores to a consolidation point or returns center. The manufacturer pays for the freight from the consolidation point to the manufacturer's returns processing facility.

The twist lies in which party actually pays the transportation carrier. Negotiating an arrangement by which the retailer pays the carrier and bills the manufacturer for the costs to move goods from the consolidation point to the manufacturer's location can usually save the manufacturer as much as twenty percent. Also, this arrangement increases the retailer's volume, which they can leverage to keep their overall transportation rates down, which in turn, helps the manufacturer as well.

The retailer also has an opportunity for profit when using this type of transaction. Many retailers incorporate an up-charge over their actual carrier rates. The manufacturer is fine with this because the rate they end up paying is still substantially lower than the rate the manufacturer pays without the retailer's help. For many retailers, this can put, literally, millions on the bottom line. The manufacturers are saving money and keeping a critical customer happy so it is a win-win for both.

Designing reverse logistics transportation networks can be challenging. If carefully developed, however, you can improve customer service while controlling costs, and minimizing transportation expenses. Transportation is a key support function that will dramatically impact the value derived from the reverse logistics ecosystem. Increases in the cost of transportation will outpace health care cost increases between now and 2020, so transportation's impact will continue to grow. While reverse logistics is less than five percent of transportation spent for most companies today, the impact on corporate earnings is material and worth focusing resources to develop and manage reverse logistics transportation services now and in the future.

Reverse Logistics Software

Today, more than ever, efficiently processing returned goods can literally be the difference between a company losing money or making money. The reverse logistics management system (RMS) used to process returns is **the** critical component of a modern reverse logistics process. The system that drives the processing of product flowing through the reverse logistics pipeline will determine if a company maximizes the value of returned assets or if these valuable assets are thrown away.

If you drew a picture of a car that represented the state of many company's reverse logistics process, it would look like Fred Flintstone's. For other, best-in-class organizations, the car looks like a Ferrari. The question is: "What differentiates a Flintstone mobile from a Ferrari?" The answer is the returns management system (RMS). Not only does the Ferrari outperform the Flintstone mobile, it enables best-in-class companies to have a five to twelve percent earnings advantage over their competitors.

While there are not many supply chain executives who have significant experience managing reverse logistics, there are even fewer information technology (IT) executives with experience. It is this lack of experience and knowledge about reverse logistics that can lead to poor decisions concerning reverse logistics software. Generally, these bad decisions begin with the buy or build choice. Many companies that decide to build a software solution instead of buying a proven reverse logistics system and tailoring it to their needs do so without understanding the complexities and differences from their existing WMS system. Flushing returns up the pipe are very different than shipping pristine product in new packaging.

It is puzzling how many very smart, and otherwise capable, executives take reverse logistics lightly. Most would never consider designing and implementing a point-of-sale system, manufacturing support, or an inventory management system. Yet, these same executives will look at reverse logistics and decide to build the solution using inexperienced, internal resources. They never question whether any of those internal resources know anything about reverse logistics.

Many years ago, I was working with an office products retailer. They were looking to buy a reverse logistics system as part of a modernization of their reverse logistics process. My team spent two days in a conference room outlining the design, the reports, and the critical information components they would need in an RMS. At the end of two days, their director of the systems team asked how much it would cost for a user's license and annual maintenance. The answer was $250,000 and $40,000 a year for maintenance. He laughed and stated that he could write a package for half that in six months using existing resources for maintenance. A couple of weeks later I learned that he had convinced the senior staff to allow him to write the program in-house. He got the green light to start coding even though, up until the two-day design meeting, he had never heard the term reverse logistics.

Anyone involved in software development will tell you that, most often, the first version of any software package will not work as advertised and writing a software application will take twice as long as you think and cost four times as much as you planned. I told the client that this would happen but they ignored our warning and moved forward.

Predictably, a year later, I received a call informing me that the IT director was no longer with the company and that his replacement was, once again, looking to buy a proven reverse logistics package. The decision to attempt a home-grown solution cost that particular company millions in wasted development expenses; in losses on returned product that was not processed efficiently; and with lower-than-industry-average recovery values. (8)

I attended an executive training workshop at Harvard Business School and worked on a case study that analyzed the pros and cons of buying existing software solutions. The lesson I took away from this case study was that if you need software--- and your company isn't the first to realize this need making you a late adopter--- it is best to buy a package and customize it. You do risk losing some competitive advantages because the software company will take lessons learned from working with you and incorporate it into their next upgrade. However, unless you are the first to develop the software, the benefits of buying a software application that has a significant install base and is managed by an experienced system team is well worth it. (8)

When it comes to reverse logistics software development, this old adage appropriately applies: "The early bird may get the worm but the second mouse will get the cheese." You don't want to be the first mouse unless you have a clear first-mover advantage.

What to Look For in an RMS

In the rest of this chapter, we will explore what to seek in a quality returns system (RMS). We will describe the critical capabilities needed in a state-of-the-art RMS, and we will explore what differentiates a state-of-the-art reverse logistics systems from lesser, "returns processing systems". We will discuss the capabilities required to facilitate receiving, sortation, processing, asset disposition, and repair processing as well as manpower management tools. We will also review capabilities needed to facilitate shipping, financial transaction processing, reconciliation, and quality assurance processes, along with visibility requirements and recommended management reports.

The Receiving Process

The RMS receiving process should accomplish two primary functions. First, it should identify and credit the "sender" of the assets for the quantity and value of each item that they shipped to the processing facility. Secondly, the receiving process must add the value of the returned item into the "inventory" of the returns processing facility. Before an item can be returned for credit, refurbished, repaired, repackaged, recycled, or sold, it has to be properly identified and recorded as received into inventory of the returns facility or location.

Many companies treat returned product as if it were of no value. Little time and effort is given to account for the product received because it is damaged or is no longer in pristine condition. This attitude, while much less prevalent today than even five years ago, costs many organizations millions of dollars in lost inventory value. Returns processing is often viewed as "garbage in, garbage out". In reality, returns are valuable assets "in" and even more valuable assets "out".

Remember, returns are not like wine. They do not get better with age. Returns are more like bananas. They rot over time and must eventually be thrown out. In a recent survey by the Aberdeen Group manufacturers said they spend between nine and fourteen percent of sales on returns. (page 9) According to the National Retail Federation, the average retailer's return rate is over eight percent of total sales. (page 5) The inventory in the reverse logistics pipeline is worth big money and deserves a dedicated system, customized design, and excellent management oversight to ensure that the value of the products are maximized and the associated risks of mishandling the returns is minimized.

To safeguard the value of returned inventory, you must have a flexible, scalable RMS with a reliable receiving system that controls and drives a quality receiving process at the front end of the returns process. The RMS should drive a process that answers the following questions when the returned goods are received:

- When did the item arrive at the facility?
- Where did the item come from?
- Who was the shipper?
- Who was the carrier?
- Is there any damage?
- Should a freight claim be filed?
- What is the SKU / Model number / Serial number or other identifying number for item identification?
- Is the asset "hazardous" or some other regulated classification?
- What is the condition of the item? (New, defective, damaged, damaged beyond repair, in original packaging, has the item been recalled and does it require quarantine or other special handling, etc.)
- What was the quantity of each SKU received?
- What is the value of each item received?
- What is the total "inventory" of the shipment that has been received?

Once this information has been gathered and recorded for each shipment, the process of crediting the shipping customer, store, or plant can take place. One of the critical differences between a RMS and a WMS is that most WMSs rely on verifying the receipt of goods against a purchase order (PO). In the world of reverse logistics, there usually isn't a PO or a similar document. Often, what you are receiving is a complete surprise. If an advance shipment notification (ASN) is received; it should not be trusted. Also, the condition of like items received can vary greatly, some will be pristine and others almost unrecognizable. You may receive an item whose parts or pieces are spread out over several pallets or in one large pallet-sized container. The condition of the individual item determines how the asset is valued and how the item flows through the reverse logistics process.

The reconciliation process is an important back-office function that relies on the RMS receiving process. The process reconciles what the sender (customer, store, branch, retailer) says was shipped, in an ASN or credit claim, versus what was physically received. One of the challenges that exists in the world of returned products is that most of the customers, stores, plants, or consumers are not properly equipped to determine the condition of the returned item. They have no way to determine the condition or the value of the returned asset based on that condition. The accuracy of goods shipped is not reliable and the preparation and packaging of the item is not sufficient to prevent additional, sometimes significant, damage during shipment. These issues will cause differences in valuation and create the need for a back-office reconciliation process that is based on the information gathered during the receiving process.

Identifying the item, determining its condition, and valuing the inventory when it arrives are critical elements that a quality RMS receiving process must have to support its needs.

Once all of this information is gathered, the process of inspecting, refurbishing, repairing, and determining the best possible disposition for each of the assets can take place. It is at this point in the process that the value of the asset is determined. Without a well-thought-out receiving process, the value of the returned assets could be incorrect when the item is received in the returns facility. This will result in reduced value recovered for the item and incorrect credit back to the customer.

After the item is received, the RMS then facilitates the sortation and inspection process for each, individual item, based on its physical condition. It is at this point in the process that you must determine how you are going to disposition the item. In the disposition process, the RMS will guide the user along a logic path to determine if an item should be returned to the OEM, repaired, liquidated, destroyed, recycled, returned to stock or donated to charity. This type of functionality does not come with your typical WMS and cannot be developed without specific, on-point, experience in reverse logistics systems design and development.

Processing

Once or twice a year, the logistics trade publications will publish a list of third-party service providers and/or logistics software companies and show a matrix of solutions offered by each company. Practically every company that appears on these lists will have the box for reverse logistics checked. However, there are fewer than a dozen companies, IN THE WORLD, that actually have a credible reverse logistics software solution. Many third-party service providers claim to offer reverse logistics solutions, but the reality is that they do not. Pretender's software does nothing more than transport, unload, and store used or returned products. This is hardly a reverse logistics solution.

What differentiates the pretenders from the contenders is their ability to process products in a timely manner in a way that maximizes the value and minimizes the risks associated with the returned assets. The processing capabilities of the RMS are the keys to realizing the value of returned assets. Processing returned goods without a quality returns management system is like running a department store without a point of sale (POS) system. It can be done, but a lot of money will be lost and it will be very difficult to maintain control of the inventory.

There are a number of companies that try to use some part of their existing WMS to process returns. This approach seldom works, for good reason. To understand why you cannot simply process returns by running a WMS process in reverse, you need to understand the basic difference between a traditional distribution operation and a returns processing operation.

In distribution, orders for new goods are placed with the OEM or distributor. A purchase order, which tells the distribution center what to expect and a general idea of when it is going to arrive, is processed. When the goods are received, they are checked in against the purchase order and stored in a predetermined location. When orders for that product are received, a pick ticket is generated and the items are picked, consolidated, loaded, and shipped to their predetermined location. Items are typically segregated by SKU; always stored in the same part of the distribution center; and picked using a repeatable process and shipped in a uniform way. What is inside of the box almost doesn't matter. Distribution centers receive, put away, pick, and ship large, medium, and small boxes to the same locations on a scheduled basis. While emergencies occur and sometimes things don't go according to plan; mostly the ship sails on smooth water.

The condition of the individual items, so long they are not clearly damaged, does not matter and is almost never checked.

Returns operation, whether centralized or decentralized, process products with a completely different set of problems in a dynamic environment. First, no one orders returns so you have no idea, really, what will have to be processed until it is sitting on the receiving dock. After the returned item has been physically received, you must account for each specific item. You must also determine the condition and profile of the item so that it can be sorted. This sorting process and the processes that follow is what will drive the value recovery in a returns process.

For example, let's say you receive a carton containing white coffee cups. Two of the cups are in the original packaging and have never been opened. One of the cups is broken in half and cannot be re-paired. Another cup appears to have been used but has no visible flaws or defects. A quality RMS will direct processing so that the first two cups are sorted and shipped to the vendor for full cost credit. The second cup is thrown away and written off. The last cup is sold on the secondary market for twenty percent of the original retail price. As you can see from this example, processing all four cups in the same way would cause problems with the vendor, create a safety issue by shipping a broken cup or create a loss of value for three of the four cups being processed.

It is an RMS's ability to identify not only the item, but also item's condition and provides for processes that will increase the value of the returned product that differentiates a quality RMS from a low-end, gatekeeping solution. This process is referred to as "disposition-ing" the item. While this might sound complicated, it is fairly simple. Remember, we discussed in a previous chapter, that there are only six possible dispositions for any product. They are:

- Returned to the vendor or OEM for credit
- Repaired or as is liquidation
- Donated to charity
- Returned to a warehouse for later redistribution
- Recycled
- Disposed of in a landfill or incinerator

There are many variations in the processes used to flow assets through any company's reverse pipeline, but there are only six different dispositions for any item. Some companies repair goods and sell them on the secondary market, for example, while others don't repair anything. They have a simple, yet important, controlled destruction process. Some new items are repackaged and stored for next season while other items are donated to charity. Some companies are very concerned about brand protection while others are much more interested in keeping costs down and getting the most for the item returned. The options and variations are as numerous as the companies and the items they sell.

Because of these possible variations, an RMS must be flexible in terms of how items may be sorted and processed in order to accommodate market demands and seasonal issues. The RMS must also have the ability to capture the information needed to ensure that the item is sorted and prepared properly to achieve the customer's goals, while minimizing the risks that might result from the potential for improper disposition of the returned item.

Receiving and processing is the first phase of an RMS and it is here that the returned assets are identified, financial transactions are triggered that transfer ownership, and the value of the returned product is determined.

The second, final phase of processing assets in the reverse logistics pipeline is the shipping process. This phase is where the cash register rings. During this phase, returned assets are removed from the company's inventory in exchange for credit toward future purchase or cash.

Shipping product from a return center is quite different from shipping product from a distribution center. In a distribution center, orders are received, picked, and prepared for shipment. The outbound process is fairly uniform and is controlled by the order picking process and transportation requirements. However, in a return center, shipping is quite different. Items are grouped for shipment based on specific vendor agreement terms and conditions, no "shipping orders", or transportation requirements. Because of the differing shipment cutoff criteria, a reverse logistics system must have several additional features that typically do not exist in a traditional warehouse management system.

The triggering mechanism to pick and ship goods in most top- tier RMSs is called the cut off criteria. Upstream in the returns process, items will have been segregated based on item condition and "return point". Each of these return points will have its own cutoff criteria. Cutoff refers to segregating processed parts or goods into pre-defined shipping quantities, based on return agreement terms and conditions. There are a few methods to cutoff returned or recalled items in a state-of-the-art RMS. They are:

- By quantity of items---cases or pallets
- By "cap" which establishes a percentage of sales that may be returned during a time period
- By value of goods that is to be shipped
- By the number of days an item has been in the returns facility

Each return point may have a unique cutoff. In addition to this unique cutoff a "global cutoff" is also established. The global cutoff is typically defined as a parameter of values, such as: ship every 30 days or every time $10,000 of product is accumulated. The RMS shipping process is set up to run through a hierarchy that looks to the individual return point cutoff criteria first and then to the global cutoff. Once one of these cutoff criteria is reached, the return authorization (RA) will be processed.

Return authorization is the process of "getting permission" from the company to whom you are going to send the returns. This notifies the receiving party of the quantity and make up of the returns shipment and establishes the basis for the financial transaction that is processed upon shipment.

Return Authorizations (RA)

There are four types of returns authorizations:

1. Call for RA – The shipper applying for credit calls the receiver who will give credit and request an RA number that will be used to track and credit the return.

2. Fax or Email for RA – Same as calling for an RA but a fax or email requesting an RA number is sent automatically by the RMS without human intervention.
3. Standing RA – An RA number is provided upfront by the receiver of the goods and is used by the sender for all outbound shipments with no additional advanced notice or approval except possibly an ASN.
4. No RA Needed – no tracking number, advanced notice, or permission needed, except, possibly, an ASN.

Requiring the shipper to request an RA can often delay credit and slow down the shipment of goods. Because of this, an RMS must have a number of RA request tracking reports that can track RA aging, RA dollars outstanding, etc. The RA process and the RA related reports are critical to keep returned product flowing smoothly through a returns facility. This part of the RMS must be very robust and flexible to ensure product is shipped and the financial claims are filed in a timely manner.

One of the most important metrics in a return center is inventory turns. The shipping process and cutoff criteria will determine the number of inventory turns a return center can achieve. A good benchmark for return center inventory turns is between twenty to thirty turns per year. This is only possible however, if the RMS has the process discipline and visibility tools to enable the user to monitor receiving, inventory, cutoffs, return authorizations, items to be picked, liquidation inventory, and the ability to ship the returns in a timely manner.

Remember, the shipping process of an RMS is where the cash register rings in the returns process. Until the point of shipping, the returns process has only cost money. You've collected a lot of broken, recalled stuff and stuff but it is still your stuff. The shipping process groups it into shipments, ships it out, and charges the receiving party for the shipment. In order to do this effectively, the RMS must have a flexible return point cutoff process, aging reports, picking logic, manifest capabilities, verification processes, and financial transaction processes built into the shipping module.

Two Types of Return Infrastructures

Before we go too much farther, it should be pointed out that there are two basic infrastructures used to process returns. One is referred to as the direct method of processing and the other is referred to as the centralized method of processing.

The direct method is when returns are processed at the point of return by the final customer and returned directly from that point to the item's final destination.

This is a decentralized design that relies on people in the field or store to prepare and ship goods. Examples of direct return processors are small retailers, field repair depot operations, and hospitals that return medical equipment parts or supplies.

The centralized method revolves around a central location where recalls and returned goods are shipped to from the field and consolidated in the centralized facility for processing. Goods are received from the field; prepped; consolidated by final destination or disposition; and shipped.

Depending upon the company and the volume of returns, the centralized method can provide significant savings and a higher quality processing. The vast majority of large high tech manufacturers, retail chains, and Internet retailers use a centralized model to process returns.

Whether an organization should use the direct or the centralized model depends upon a number of factors that ultimately determine a balance between cost of processing and recovery value. These factors include:

- Volume of returns
- Disposition of returned assets
- Residual value of returns
- Number of field or store locations
- Labor required to process returns
- Risk from processing errors
- Regulatory risks
- Existing field systems

- Cost of centralized facilities
- Transportation costs
- Supporting corporate infrastructure

RMS Visibility Requirements

Whether a company has a centralized model that relies on an RMS for processing and visibility tools or use a direct model that relies on a point-of-sale system or some other back office application to process returns, the visibility requirements are quite similar. Having easy access to meaningful information enables the reverse logistics executive to monitor and manage the returns process and the assets flowing through the reverse logistics pipeline.

The following is a list of reports or visibility requirements every state-of-the-art reverse logistics system should include. The actual format may vary based on the company, but the basic needs will be there. The list below is broken down by function, with a brief explanation.

Receiving

- Advanced shipment notification – receipts in transit by date, store/field/customer, carrier
- Receipts by store/field location/customer - by receiving, RMA, month, quarter, year
- Returns by SKU/Category/OEM – by RMA, month, quarter, year
- All reports should show quantity and value per unit and in total
- Exception reporting comparing ASNs and actual product received

Processing

- Total units processed – by day, week, month, quarter, year

- Units received and processed by disposition – Return to OEM, liquidated, repaired, restocked, donated, recycled, destroyed – by day, week, month, quarter, year
- Manpower reports showing hours worked within each function
- Through Put – In returns facilities through put is typically calculated as follows: Total Units Received / Total Variable Hours

Shipping

- Shipments waiting for return authorization – by date, value, quantity
- Pick tickets outstanding
- Hazardous material manifests ready for shipment – by class
- Manifests – by date, OEM, liquidator, recycler, charity
- Liquidated product awaiting shipment
- Inventory turns

Quality Assurance

- Inbound receipt verification
- Cycle inventory
- Physical inventory – in total, by OEM, category, dollar, units
- Process verification – by function, employee, month, quarter, year
- Location verification – by type of location: bulk, rack, flow rack, shelf, security, day, week, month, quarter year
- Outbound verification – by OEM, liquidator, hazardous shipments, recalled/regulated shipments, random manifest

When it comes to visibility there are endless variations for each type of report listed above. The first RMS installed in Walmart's Bentonville, Arkansas Returns Center, fondly referred to as "8098", had a grand total of twenty-six reports. (8) Cutting edge at the time, these reports provided a great deal of value to buyers, store operations, and the facility management team. Times have changed and so have expectations. Today the average RMS will have well over 100 reports initially available and many now incorporate an easy to use report writer that will allow the user to develop an endless list of custom or one-time reports. There is no magical number of reports.

Today, best-in-class reverse logistics systems offer all reports via the Internet and can be accessed from anywhere in the world. Modern-day solutions offer reports by facility, by region, country, and in total. The potential variety of reports is limitless. It is the reporting capabilities and visibility tools that provide the information needed to drive value to the bottom line in the reverse logistics process.

As with all reporting, however, reverse logistics executives should be careful not to get too caught up in developing new reports or constant re-formatting of existing reports. Visibility is only valuable when decisions are being made that impact the business in a positive manner. There is nothing to be gained by having ten new reports that no one in your organizations uses or even understands.

Over the next five years, every company will be forced to rethink their existing reverse logistics network, infrastructure, and supporting systems. As the cost of transportation continues to escalate, the cost of processing will drive dramatic changes in disposition.

The decisions caused by these changes in cost structures must rely on quality data that comes from an organization's reverse logistics system. This system will be your only source of accurate data needed to analyze and revise existing returns networks and will be critical in maximizing the value of returned assets and associated risks in the future.

Reverse Logistics Software Providers

The following list reverse logistics software (RMS) providers we compiled over 2010 and 2011. We hope this list is helpful to those companies interested in purchasing reverse logistics software from established RMS providers. Each of these providers has their own area of expertise. Their capabilities vary greatly depending on their target markets and areas of expertise. Some offer standalone systems while others only offer their reverse logistics software as part of a broader service offering. As with all large capital purchases be sure to do your homework and select your RMS provider carefully. Remember **caveat emptor** - buyers beware.

Company	Web Address
4CS iWarranty	4cs.com
Accellos	accellos.com
Aljex Software	aljex.com
AndSoft	and-soft.com
Andlor	andlor.com
Bar Control	barcontrol.com

Company	Web Address
Cadre Technologies	cadretech.com
CDC Software Corp	cdcsoftware.com
Clear Orbit	clearorbit.com
Click Commerce	clickcommerce.com
CT Logistics	ctlogistics.com
CTSI-Global	ctsi-global.com
Datex	datexcorp.com
DEX	dex.com
The ECN Group	ecngroup.com.au
Elemica	elemica.com
Entigo	entigo.com
Epicor Software	epicor.com
Fast Design	fast-design.com
Fortigo	fortigo.com
Freightgate	freightgate.com
Fulcrum	fulcrumwarranty.com
Genco	genco.com
Green Oak Solutions	greenoaksolutions.com
Infor	infor.com
Inmar Inc	inmar.com
InMotion Global	inmotionglobal.com
INSIGHT	insightoutsmart.com
Intelliset	intelliset.com
JDA Software Group	jda.com
Kewill	kewill.com
Logistics Management Solutions	lmslogistics.com

Company	Web Address
Log-Net	log-net.com
LogFire	logfire.com
Logistix Solutions	logistixsolutions.com
Magaya Corporations	magaya.com
Manhatten Associates	manh.com
Metrix	metrix.com
Microsoft Dynamics	microsoft.com/dynamics
Company	**Web Address**
ModusLink	moduslink.com
Newgistics	newgistics.com
NTE	nte.com
One Network Enterprises	onenetwork.com
Oracle	oracle.com
RateLinx	ratelinx.com
Return Goods	returngoods.com
Return Incorporated	returninc.com
Royal 4 Systems	royal4.com
SAP	sap.com
SAS	sas.com
Service Central	servicecentral.com
Servigistics	servigistics.com
Smart Software	smartcorp.com
Sterling Commerce	sterlingcommerce.com
Supply Vision	supply-vision.com
Supply Chain Alliance	supplychainalliance.com
Tavant	tavant.com
Transite Technology	transite.com
TransportGistics	transportgistics.com
Ultra Logistics	ultrashiptms.com
XCaliber Technologies	xcalibertech.com

The world of reverse logistics is getting more complex every day. There are many companies exploring solutions to meet the need of manufacturers, retailers, and distributors. It is important to identify those few providers that have the market experience, customer references, and capabilities to truly add value to your reverse logistics process.

We recommend selecting a dozen or so possible RMS providers and include them in a Request For Information (RFI). Once you get the basic information, you should conduct phone interviews, reference checks, and possibly short face-to-face presentations. Then, cull down the group to six or fewer and send out a more detailed RFP.

Review the responses and conduct phone reviews with the providers. From this group, select three possible candidates and schedule a presentation that includes a demo of the software and a tour of an existing client that utilizes the software. During the selection process, look for a culture fit, comfort with the providers' approaches to change management, support, maintenance, and of course, total cost. After the process is concluded, you will have more than enough information to select your provider.

CHAPTER 10

Repair and Refurbishment

In the 1990s, retailers and high tech manufacturers, often used the term "convergence" when discussing the future of consumer technology. Convergence was defined as the merging of two or more separate electronics into one. For example, combining a calculator, electronic Rolodex, computer, and a cell phone into what we know today as an IPhone.

Those who predicted convergence were correct; and today, convergence has gone mainstream. We have cell phones that are also computers, contact lists, global positioning systems and more. Household appliances have significant intelligence built into them. Televisions are high definition and "on demand" is to watch movies, shows, and play games at the consumer's whim.

As a result of this explosion of technology, the value of reverse logistics has grown. But the converged products we use today, are just the tip of the convergence iceberg. Over the next twenty years, as resources dwindle, the ability to test, repair, refurbish, and re-manufacture returns will become a vital function for every manufacturer or retailer of electronics, household appliances, and white goods.

As an industry, repair service is still in its infancy. There are thousands of repair shops but no dominant player that can claim even a modest market share. As the importance of test and repair processes increase, we expect to see clear leaders in the field emerge.

The repair service business is a difficult one. Finding a qualified company to provide a high-quality repair service at an affordable cost while producing an acceptable yield can be a real challenge. In the mid 1990s there were roughly a dozen well-known repair service providers in North America. (8) All but two of those service providers have gone bankrupt.

Using a repair service provider that subsequently files for bankruptcy protection, can lead to big trouble. Depending on the contract language; how the financial transactions for service have been processed; and who is responsible for purchasing new packaging and parts, you could be forced to pay all outstanding invoices and get no product in return.

The point is, that you must be careful not to shortcut the due diligence required in selecting a vendor. You must not only be sure they can provide the quality and cost-effective repair service but that they are financially sound as well. You should be wary of any provider that has a single, dominant customer unless it is your company. Think about what could happen if they lose that customer. How will it impact you if they are your sole repair service provider?

Contract Recommendations

The contract between your company and the service provider should include protection from a bankruptcy. While you can never be fully protected, you can reduce these risks. We are not attorneys, this is not a legal opinion, and as with all contracts, you should consult a legal expert before signing. However, over the years we have seen companies protect themselves from taking a major financial hit from bankrupt service providers. A good way to do protect your company from the potential damage of a bankruptcy filing by a repair service provider is to require financial terms incorporating the following recommendations:

- As the service provider receives product, charge them for the goods, effectively requiring them to buy the entire product at a predetermined price. This protects you if your service provider closes up and disappears in the middle of the night.
- While the service provider processes, tests, and repairs all of the returned products, you will buy back only the repaired items at a predetermined price. This shifts the risk of poor testing and yield rates where it belongs, on the shoulders of the repair company.
- The repair company should be solely responsible for the purchase of packaging and parts. In some instances, where there are common parts used on a regular basis, you might want to buy those parts directly; but unless you are proficient at parts management, leave the parts procurement to the provider.
- The repair service provider should build parts costs into the purchase price. As a general rule, and this can vary greatly depending on the items being repaired, new parts should only account for about fifteen percent of the parts used in repairing consumer goods. The other eighty-five of the parts will come from other scrapped units.

When selecting a service provider, your field of possible candidates will require some critical information in order for them to accurately price their services and submit a bid.

Answering the following list of questions before talking to the service providers is good preparation and it will help you judge the real contenders from the mere pretenders.

REPAIR SERVICES QUESTIONNAIRE

1. What is the estimated volume of returns that will be received?
2. What is the estimated number of units that will be tested?
3. What is the anticipated failure rate of items that are tested? (Percentage)
4. What is the estimated number of units to be repaired?
5. Describe the various warranty programs, percentage of returns by category, and length of time for each program.
6. Do you offer extended warranty programs and if so, please describe the various programs and who administers the program?
7. Do you use any repair software applications? If yes, please describe.
8. Describe the types of proprietary parts that are to be used in the repair process, how are the parts to be sourced, along with any secondary suppliers, limitations, or other pertinent data?
9. May failed units be cannibalized for parts?
10. Who will be responsible for procuring new parts used for repair?
11. Are replacement parts available from the OEM?
12. Provide a list of approved parts suppliers.
13. Describe the packaging requirement for each class of repaired and refurbished goods.
14. Are electrostatic discharge (ESD) bags required for all products?
15. Who is responsible for procurement of the ESD bags?
16. What are the service level agreements for receipt, testing, repair, and refurbishment of goods?
17. Do you have an advanced exchange program?
18. What are the response times for advanced exchange?
19. Describe outbound packaging requirements for each class of goods repaired and refurbished.
20. Describe any required certifications or training for repair technicians.
21. What are the _____(KPI) and other measurements that you will use in judging the performance of the service provider?

Depending on the market segment and variety of products that are to be repaired, the service provider may ask for a sampling of items to work through in order to price their services. Many companies that outsource repair services are hesitant to do this. They usually think that, if the service provider really knows what it is doing, a dry run should not be needed. We disagree; and believe that this is an important step that will enable your providers to give you the more accurate pricing.

With the speed of change in the world of electronics, sampling real returns and running them through the process will ensure a quality quote from the service provider. Forcing any third-party service provider to blindly bid, based on a handful of self-made assumptions, is asking for trouble in the relationship and ultimately, will result in higher costs.

It is not unusual for companies that force this type of bidding process on their third parties to find themselves paying more for the services than budgeted. The relationship between the two parties is strained and it makes everyone look and feel bad.

Once you have selected a short list of repair service providers, you should tour their locations and talk to three or more existing customers. Make a concerted effort really work to confirm that the provider is competent.

Another way to determine if a potential service provider is a contender or pretender is to find out how well they manage parts. Many repair companies have gone out of business because they have done a poor job of managing parts.

If a repair company is going to test and repair inventory, they should plan to obtain a certain number of parts from failed units. The question is how many parts will be taken from failed units and how many new parts will be purchased.

The theory behind parts management is straightforward, but due to the number of parts, actually managing parts can be a challenge. There are a number of software applications that are specifically designed for parts management. Whether a service provider uses one of these applications or has an in-house system does not matter as long as they have an effective process and use it religiously.

Examine parts management and what percentage of parts can be cannibalized from failed units. Compare this conclusion to the expected failure rates during the testing process. Taken together, do these two assumptions make sense?

Next, think about the source for new parts. Are there any restrictions on buying certified parts from a particular OEM? If the service provider is buying parts on the open market without any restrictions, do they have back-up parts providers, if needed? If a major parts supplier can't fill the orders for some reason, you must have a back up supplier to keep the process running smoothly. Remember, electronics lose ten percent of the recovery value ever month they sit on the shelf. Be certain that the repair providers service guarantees the speedy processing of all products.

Repair-service providers may also need to have warranty existing repair agreements in order to repair your returned products. While in many industries this is a standard requirement, do not assume that just because a repair company is a certified warranty repair shop that they know what they are doing. Also, do not assume that a certified warranty shop can procure name-brand parts more quickly than anyone else.

In the mid 1990s we were working for a number of clients that were getting a substantial number of personal computers (PCs) returned. In order to provide a better overall service offering, we explored partnering with a PC repair company. We searched the market and identified three possible partners.

We selected one of the candidates because they were certified warranty repair specialists for literally every PC manufacturer in the world. This would give us the leverage to liquidate product at a much higher recovery and offer an extended warranty on top.

What we didn't understand was at that time; PC manufacturers would certify just about any company that asked if they could show a minimum level of repair capabilities. If you could hold a screwdriver, fill out the application properly, and followed up on your request, you were going to get your certification.

The other critical thing we did not understand was that, in order to repair the popular brands under warranty and to offer extended warranties when liquidating the repaired units, we had to use name brand parts.

The problem with this was that the manufacturers only made enough parts to build new units and had very few spare parts available for repair purposes. They are, after all, in the business of selling new machines. Thus, we had huge backlogs of PC waiting for name brand parts that were coming from the manufacturers, who saw our services as direct competition. If you bought a refurbished PC you were not going to buy a new PC.

Do you know what you call a $2,000 PC waiting for a name brand keyboard and mouse? A boat-anchor. After about ninety days, the recovery value no longer covered the cost of processing and repair.

We took care of our customers to make sure they didn't get hurt and got out of the repair business as fast as we could. Today, every one of the repair companies we considered partnering with is out of business. Some went out of business because of bad management and others went out of business because their processes became obsolete. Many repair companies struggle at deciding what equipment to buy. This has a direct impact on what sectors they can service. (14)

For example, if a repair company is going to repair laptop motherboards, they need a special piece of equipment that is, in effect, a microscopic welder. This piece of equipment costs about $250,000 (8); and if they do any volume at all, the repair company will need to have four or five of them. If the price of a motherboard drops dramatically, they could see their market vanish because their customers could buy a new motherboard less expensively than they could repair a used one.

This has happened to a number of repair vendors who invested heavily in equipment to test and repair cathode ray tubes (CRTs). When flat-panel screens began to dominate the market, their business disappeared.

Levels of Repair

There are three basic levels of repair.

- Level I – Reformat Software
- Level II – Component Replacement
- Level III – Core Repair

From a service provider's standpoint, think of Level I as taking two hours to repair; Level II, two days; and Level III, two weeks.

Because of the level of complexity, equipment required, and technical training required, most repair companies only provide Level I and II repairs.

In fact, unless the item has a high post-repair resale value, Level III repairs do not make any sense for either the customer, or the third-party repair provider. Items that require Level III are usually scrapped for parts and recycled or sold "as is" on the secondary market.

In today's ever changing, unpredictable, high tech world, speed and flexibility are critical. What makes sense to fix and resell today may lose money tomorrow. Your network must be comprised of specialists who can repair the product quickly, maximize the yield, and provide a cost-effective service. Avoid long-term commitments and always think in terms of net, realizable profit.

CHAPTER 11

How Centralized Return
Centers Operate

Centralized return centers are warehouse facilities used to consolidate and process recalled and returned inventory. Centralizing and processing returns started in the grocery industry. Grocery chains developed and adopted centralized returns because of their razor-thin margins and even smaller earnings. Grocers were forced to leave no stone unturned when it came to reducing costs and saving money.

The first major non-grocery company to centralize returns was Walmart Stores in the early 1980s. At the time, this was just one of many ways Walmart lowered operating costs. The majority of general merchandise retailers in North America adopted centralized returns processing during the 1990s and early 2000s.

Major manufacturers were not far behind. With the development of Internet-based retail formats and the expansion of catalog retailing, centralized returns processing became a best practice everyone wanted and needed to adopt in order to control costs and satisfy their customers. While consolidating returns has won wide acceptance, few people understand how these facilities function.

What NOT to Process Through a Centralized Return Center

Before we talk about how a centralized return center actually operates, let's discuss some products that should not be processed there. Not every category of product in a retail store, or in a manufacture's assortment should be processed centrally through a return center. There are a few product categories that should not be processed centrally because of their hazardous nature or regulatory restrictions, processing these products centrally will actually cost more money and significantly increase potential liability and risk.

As a general rule, the following categories should **NOT** be processed through a central returns facility:

- Pool chemicals and other similar oxidizers
- Pesticides
- Car batteries or similar products
- Firearms, ammunitions, or explosives - Firearms and ammunitions are usually centralized in a special, high- security returns facility, monitored by the federal government.
- Pharmaceuticals – Similar to firearms, controlled pharmaceuticals returns are centralized but they are sent to separate, high security, facilities that are closely monitored by the FDA and the U.S. Drug Enforcement Administration (DEA).

The manufacturers and wholesalers for the five categories above have developed store-level or branch programs that are designed to provide pickup, transportation, and processing of their products flowing through the reverse logistics pipeline.

While the costs for processing these items directly from a store or branch can be higher when compared to other centralized processing costs, the vast majority of organizations that receive, process, and ship these products agree that the trade- off in reduced liability and lower risk is well worth the increased cost.

Return Center Process Flow

The return center process flow, illustrated on the last page of this chapter, shows the typical layout of a return center. Before we get into the nuts and bolts of how a return center operates, there are a few things to keep in mind.

First, a return center is NOT a warehouse or distribution center. That is to say, the purpose of a return center is not to store returns. Return centers are processing facilities. They are used to receive, sort, test, repair, package, consolidate and ship recalled goods or customer returns. They are flow-through facilities not storage locations.

Return centers cannot be designed to hold returns due to the variability of the returns. Unlike a distribution centers, returns are not ordered from a manufacturer or distributor. Generally, the contents of a trailer filled with returns is unknown. While one can predict certain things at a high level, it is virtually impossible to predict any granular detail of inbound receipts for a return center.

The second reason why return centers are not holding facilities is that returns lose value the longer they are held. Returns are not like fine wine. They do not improve or increase in value with age. In fact, many returns tend to lose about ten percent of their retail value for every month they are held. You must move returns through the return process to their final disposition as quickly as possible. For every business day that returned inventory sits in your facility, it could lose up to one half of one percent in value. (8) Because of these drivers, a good return center will turn their inventory twenty-five to thirty times a year or more. (14)

The physical flow of product through a return center is uniform throughout industries. The following chart outlines the flow of product through a centralized return center by area and function:

Area	Function
Inbound Receiving	Unload inbound trucks; receive pallets and small parcel shipments.
Scanning	Enter units into the returns management system or manually record each unit. This is the point of transferring ownership and where product is added to the return center inventory and the time to reconcile physical units to financial charges.
Primary Sortation	High volume units are sorted to pallets according to final disposition such as return to vendor, liquidation, etc.
Repair Area	Designated items are tested and repaired. Units that cannot be repaired are scrapped and recycled while usable parts or rare, earth minerals are collected, saved, and used to repair or manufacture other units.
Flow Rack Sortation	Flow rack or shelf sort area for small cube items. Product sorted by final destination address.
Bulk Storage	Area for large items that are too big for fixed rack area. Product will be sorted by final destination address.
Fixed Rack Locations	Lower level slot locations are used to sort case pack items. Upper level used to re-warehouse full pallets from fixed and flow rack areas.
Recycling Area	Area where products are sorted, broken down and prepared for shipment to recyclers.
Dumpster	Trash compactor / bailer for packaging and product disposal.

Area	Function
Outbound Shipping	Area where product is staged for shipping. Outbound manifests are reconciled to shipments and shipments are loaded on outbound trailers.

Return Center Facility Process Flow

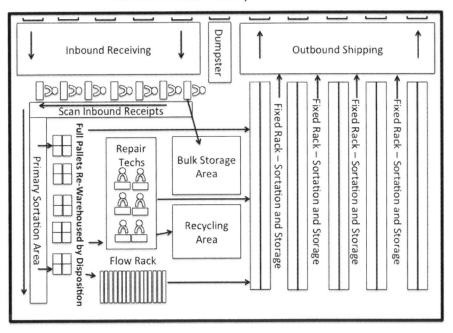

CHAPTER 12

Christmas Returns

MERRY CHRISTMAS! Not so much in the reverse logistics industry. The impact of reverse logistics is never felt more than during the Christmas returns season. For retailers, the Christmas returns season begins in mid December, followed by a veritable tsunami of returns that arrive beginning the first week of January and continues through February, to the first week of March. For manufacturers of consumer goods, Christmas returns start to flow during the first week of January ramping up to full volume by the third week in January and lasting through March.

The volume spikes for manufacturers are the same as their retail counterparts. The only difference is that the manufacturers have a slight delay while the retailers process the holiday volume.

The good news for reverse logistics team members is that they usually get to take some time off around Christmas while their brothers and sisters in the distribution and retail world live at work. The bad news is that after New Years, for many they will not get to take a weekend off until spring.

If you look at the chart below, you will see how return volumes varies between general merchandise (GM) retailers, Internet retailers, and food retailers. You will also notice that the chart begins in September, which is usually the slowest month of the year for reverse logistics volume. The first quarter peak is obvious and requires special planning and scheduling, which is be addressed further in this book.

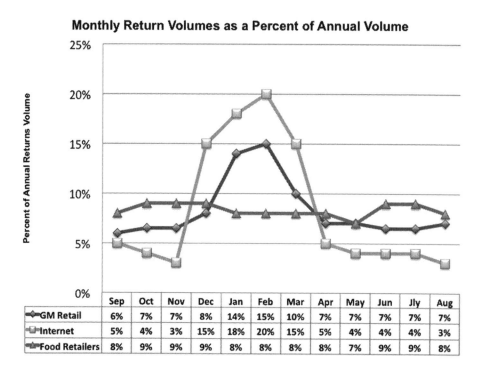

Monthly Return Volumes as a Percent of Annual Volume

	Sep	Oct	Nov	Dec	Jan	Feb	Mar	Apr	May	Jun	Jly	Aug
GM Retail	6%	7%	7%	8%	14%	15%	10%	7%	7%	7%	7%	7%
Internet	5%	4%	3%	15%	18%	20%	15%	5%	4%	4%	4%	3%
Food Retailers	8%	9%	9%	9%	8%	8%	8%	8%	7%	9%	9%	8%

Planning for the Christmas Returns Season

The key to surviving the Christmas returns season is preparation. While you will not know exactly what items you will be unloading from the trailer, you should be able to have a fairly good idea of the unit volume, plus or minus ten percent--which is as good as it gets in the world of reverse logistics.

Remember, one of the biggest differences between distribution operations and reverse logistics is that the inbound volume in a DC is predictable. It is based on a pre-determined group of items, for which specific purchase orders have been cut, and products are received on specific receiving documents. Distribution center managers can predict, down to the unit and SKU, what will be arriving and on what day it will arrive.

In the return center, all that you know is that there will be inbound freight to unload. You will not know exactly what the products will be because it is based on what the consumer returns and what didn't sell as planned. In addition, you have no idea what condition the products are. As you recall, returned items are handled in one of only six ways, depending upon the condition of the item at the time of receipt. You must be prepared for anything. Planning is essential. But remember, it is a poor plan that can't be modified.

Seasonal Recalls or Guaranteed Sales Returns

Seasonal recalls lend a little more stability to Christmas returns planning. For many retailers and manufacturers, end-of-the- season recalls can be sixty percent or more of the total volume processed in the first quarter.

Most consumers don't realize that most, if not all, of the unsold toasters, and coffee makers with Christmas symbols printed on the outside of the package are pulled from store shelves and returned to a return facility where they are repackaged and shipped back to stores as normal, non-seasonal, product.

Many categories, such as automotive; housewares; and health and beauty aids manufacturers pull many SKUs for repackaging as well. In December, much of the packaging has a red background. In January, it all turns blue. Of course, this is also the time of the year when you clear out the remnants of the out-going season to make room for the next season's hottest selling items. This practice is referred to as seasonal recalls or call backs.

Buyers and merchants decide what they are going to recall in early December and are usually fairly accurate when predicting SKUs and volumes. Because of this, it is important for the vice president of reverse logistics to stay in close communication with the buyers and merchants regarding their recall plans for end-of-season merchandise.

Once reasonable estimates are established on return volumes due to customer returns and recall volumes, the most critical part of the Christmas returns season is addressed---developing a manpower plan.

Manpower Planning

The basic framework for a manpower plan should be established early November and be flexible enough to adjust for surprises in the recall area. By early November, the following pieces should be in place:

- Base staffing – how many employees are needed on each shift, and from where will they be hired
- Leadership – how many supervisors needed for all shifts
- How many temporary workers are needed, by shift, and which temp services will be used during the peak season
- How will temporary supervisors, employees on loan, and other temporary workers be trained
- How much extra storage space is required and what is the plan for leasing or acquiring the temporary space and/or outside storage trailers

Once a basic outline of a working plan in place, the details can be filled in. Following, are some guidelines to help detail a working plan.

If possible, base staffing should be sixty to seventy percent company employees. Thirty to forty percent subsequently are hired from temporary service providers. We recommend that if possible, using a greater percentage of temporary employee is more desirable. Existing distribution centers are a ready source for employees, if your company has a DC in close proximity to the return center. As return centers hit their peak, the distribution process is slowing down.

At the Walmart return center in Bentonville, we usually had between two to three hundred Walmart Associates from the surrounding DCs who helped us get through the high volume returns months. We opened up the jobs for volunteers and there were always more than enough DC associates who wanted the overtime or were just looking to change up their work environment. (8)

Temporary Leadership

Temporary leadership is also critical for peak season success. We recommend looking to existing lead employees to fill these positions. If using employees from neighboring DCs, extra supervisors can be recruited. One of the biggest mistakes that companies make while processing peak-season returns is that they do not get enough supervision to effectively manage the higher number of associates.

If this occurs, chaos can ensue. Keep in mind that you have a number of employees doing jobs that they have never done before. You usually have more people working more closely together, this can turn into a gossip fest or a little Peyton Place if your not paying attention. Do not short cut supervision.

Temporary Employees and Temp Services

When making arrangements for temporary workers, be sure to have at least two temporary services on call. A more competitive price and a greater chance of getting the number of required workers will result when, in February, employees tire of working overtime and temps just stop reporting for work.

It is also advisable to negotiate for a supervisor from the temp service to take attendance at every shift. The temp service supervisor shows up, takes roll, and if there are missing people, quickly brings in replacements with a phone call to the agency. This can saves the return center management team headaches and allows them to get the returns processing engine running rather than chasing down replacement, temporary workers.

Once the organizational chart for each shift is complete, a training plan is required. We recommend having the temporary supervisors shadow existing supervisors for one to two weeks prior to the returns season. They don't need to know all that there is to know about management. They simply need to know the basics of taking attendance, keeping the team moving, how to do the job they are supervising and when to call for help.

Hourly associates, temporary or on loan, they should only need two or three days of training time with other employees to learn their jobs. Keep it simple and assign them to a mentor employee.

While determining shift schedules, work with the management team to ensure that experienced employees are spread throughout all shifts. Paying a shift differential or premium may be required to place experienced temporary employees where they are needed, but this is money well spent.

Because of the huge spikes in volume, many return centers go from one shift, five-day-a-week operation, to three shifts, six or seven days a week. Even with this level of commitment, it can be difficult to keep the volume under control.

While calculating the number of people needed per shift, don't fall into the trap of simply dividing everything by two or three. Increasing from a one shift to a two shift operation, expect the first shift to do about sixty percent of all the work and one hundred percent of the more technical work such as completing shipping paperwork, processing hazardous material disposal, processing recycling, researching unknown items, and other similarly complex tasks.

Often, the first shift tees up a lot of work for the second shift. From a high-level metrics view point, this can give the appearance of higher productivity on second shift than first shift but one could not succeed without the preparation completed by the other. Keep that in mind when evaluating performance.

When planning workload, be sure to involve the reverse logistics team and make sure that the complex, critical steps are taken addressed by trained, trustworthy employees---or make alternative plans.

Space

The last step in preparing for Christmas returns season is to ensure sufficient operating space. This is another area that companies try to save money on---only to regret it in February.

There are usually three options for additional space. The first place to look is within existing, local distribution centers. Distribution center volume is generally at its lowest in January and space is often available.

The second option is to rent storage trailers. These are not road worthy trailers but work great for holding unprocessed, inbound freight or processed outbound freight that is waiting for return authorization. Prices for, water-proof storage trailers can range from one to two hundred dollars per trailer, per month.

The number of trailers needed depends on how much extra space is needed and whether freight can be floor stacked, double stacked on pallets, or single stacked on pallets. Storage trailers are great if a few hundred trailers are needed for four to six weeks. If more freight is present and trailers are needed for more than six weeks, consider leasing off-site warehouse space on a temporary basis.

While leasing off-site facilities on a temporary basis is often a requirement during peak season, it can be an expensive resolution to the space problem. Proper planning will dictate procurement of additional space at least sixty days prior to occupation.

Security is a critical element to proper planning for Christmas returns processing. Returns are valuable and a functioning alarm system is a must. Before the temporary warehouse is used for anything, the loss prevention department should complete a security check of the entire building; make arrangements for guard service if needed; test alarm and sprinkler systems; and have all the locks on the doors changed.

While the same high, security levels in place in your returns facility are not needed, simple sign-in and sign-out sheets for employees are necessary. It is best to restrict which employees can go to the off-site location. Never allow anyone other than a qualified member of management to have the keys to open or lock up the building.

Christmas returns season is when the reverse logistic team is most valuable to the organization. As shown in the pervious chart in this chapter, many returns facilities will process forty percent or more of their entire year's volume over a sixty-day period. This type of concentrated volume, places the returns management team in a potentially heroic position. They cannot afford to take their eye off the ball. As my former boss at Walmart would say: "Execute or be executed."

Metrics

Key metrics that must be closely monitored include:

- New, inbound volume (trailers, pallets, cases, units, etc.)
- Total inbound volume not processed (backlog)
- Units processed
- Units repaired
- Shipments waiting for RA, by vendor, by value and volume
- Shipments with RAs received but not picked
- Shipments staged, waiting for loading
- Completed shipments
- Processing accuracy
- Cycle inventory results
- Inventory of supplies and parts, if applicable
- Inventory on storage trailers and/or off-site locations
- Standard productivity metrics
- Hours worked without a lost time accident

The actual metrics that will need to be tracked depends on the product, the process, and the technology used within the returns center. These metrics should be tracked by area, by shift, by day, and with rolling monthly totals that can be compared to the return center budget and Christmas returns plan.

CHAPTER 13

How To Reduce Retail
Customer Returns

The absolute, number one, best way to reduce the cost of processing returns is to reduce the amount of product that is returned by customers. Implementing strategies that actually reduce customer return rates is perhaps the closest thing to the Holy Grail in reverse logistics. It is usually the first thing executives bring up when discussing what to do about returns and usually the last thing addressed.

When faced with the challenge of actually reducing consumer return rates, the natural reaction of many executives is to tighten the customer return policy. While this does reduce the amount of product returned, it also may greatly reduce total sales. In fact, a study conducted by the Massachusetts Institute of Technology (MIT) Sloan School of Management found that while a lenient return policy does tend to increase the volume of items returned, it also reduces the ratio of returns to sales. (page 85) Many customers view a lenient return policy as one way to mitigate the risk of buying so they tend to buy more and return more items but the returns are a smaller percentage of total purchases.

If you look at examples of companies that have adjusted their customer return policies over the years, the conclusions are clear. Restricting customer return policies does much more to reduce SALES than it does to reduce the percentage of product returned. If reducing customer returns is the goal, the answer clearly is **not** to make your customer return policy more restrictive. There are more effective steps that can be taken that actually will reduce customer return rates and they all happen to be much more customer friendly, which, in turn, increases sales.

The specific steps needed to reduce customer return rates can be quite different depending on whether you are a manufacturer or a retailer, what items are being returned, how you sell your products and the market in which you compete.

For example, online sales of women's clothing have a much higher rate of return than does a brick and mortar automotive parts store. The difference is what is being sold, who is buying the product, the standardization of the product, and customer expectations. These are all critical factors influencing the rate of customer returns.

Retail Return Rates by Category

The following return rates, provided by the National Retail Federation (NRF), show the significant differences in return rates by retail category. (13 page 10)

NRF Retail Category Return Rates

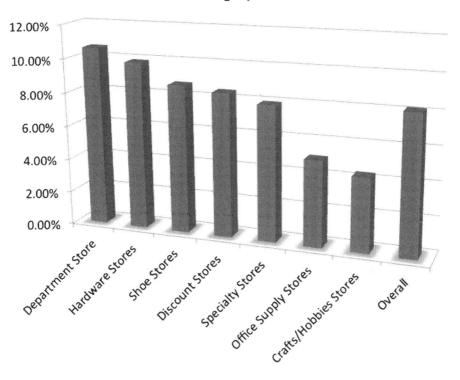

The reasons for return at a high level are generally the same. The following chart based on research conducted by Babcox Research, it shows that the reasons for return for both retail stores, and in this case an automotive ships are very similar. (15)

Reason for Returns from Shops

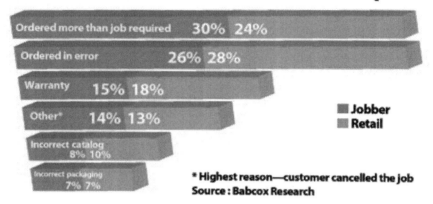

Ordered more than job required   30% 24%

Ordered in error   26% 28%

Warranty   15% 18%

Other*   14% 13%

Incorrect catalog
8% 10%

Incorrect packaging
7% 7%

■ Jobber
■ Retail

* Highest reason—customer cancelled the job
Source : Babcox Research

Across every industry and product group regardless of whether the product is industrial or consumer goods, the most common reason for making a return is some form of customer remorse. Returns due to customer remorse occur for a number of reasons including the customer duplicating an order, they may have received two red ties for Christmas, or they simply decided they did not want the item.

According to the NRF, United States consumers returned over $194 billion in 2010. Of this, $17.7 billion resulted from fraud and abuse. Other studies have shown that only twenty percent or $40 billion of consumer returns are actually defective from a manufacturers point of view.

In order to reduce customer returns, different programs are needed to combat fraud and abuse, apart from the other causes for a return.

Combating Returns Fraud

The largest, single action step that a retailer can take to combat fraud is to simply open the returned package prior to authorizing credit for the returned item. Confirming that the item is actually in the package and includes all the parts and accessories will significantly reduce fraud. It's simple and effective. Many companies make broad sweeping, changes that impact all customers not just those who cheat and steal.

Steps You Can Take To Reduce Returns

Clearly, the steps company's take to reduce the twenty percent of defective returns is completely different than actions taken to reduce fraud and abuse. This is equally true for the remaining seventy percent of returns that is neither defective nor fraudulent. The biggest opportunity to have a real impact on return rates is to focus efforts on reducing this largest percentage group, returns that are neither defective nor fraudulent.

There are three, equally important, areas that should be considered as illustrated in the chart below:

Reducing Return Rates

As we stated before, each item and each market may require different steps to impact the rate of return. There is no quick fix or one-size-fits-all solution when it comes to managing returns. This is true for the process, the policies, and certainly for the steps required to reduce the amount of inventory that is being returned.

The first step in reducing the return rate is to identify the top twenty items returned by dollar value. Once you have the top twenty identified, organize them by product category or some other common inventory attribute.

For more complex items that may require instructions and/or user guides to operate, get a copy of the instructions / user guides and read them. Many of them are very poorly written; making it no surprise that the product is frequently returned! Take a new item home and ask your spouse to put the item together or use it. Select several items and ask another person to assemble or operate them, using the instructions. Do not help, just observe and take good notes.

Next, look at the troubleshooting section. Where is the trouble shooting section? Is it easy to find? Is it easy to read? Does it make sense? Again, take good notes.

If there is a help line; call it. We once worked for a client who sold a household appliance that had to be mounted on the side of the customer's house. When we called the toll free help line, a recording that said that the help desk hours were from 9:00 a.m. to 4:00 p.m., Monday through Friday. Our client was very surprised to learn that their help line had limited hours of operation. Their typical customer would install the product after work or on the weekend, a time when phone support was unavailable. Expanding the hours the help desk was available simple, effective solution to reduce return rates.

If items are packaged in a box, put flyers in the box that provide clear instructions to customers for common mistakes or answers to frequently-asked questions. Make the troubleshooting information easy to find. Troubleshooting information doesn't mean it should be a lot of trouble to find or understand. If instructions and guides are difficult to find, read, or follow, return rates climb. Simplify the instructions; do not use technical jargon; use pictures and examples to illustrate instructions; and provide all written material in a multi-lingual format.

Packaging and labeling is also an area that is frequently overlooked as a potential source of returns. A picture speaks a thousand words. Consumers' expectations of the product's performance are clearly influences by the pictures and language used on the product's packaging. If a perfect oval loaf of bread is displayed on the bread maker's box, the customer's expectation has risen to that vision. If the vision is unattainable with the use of the product, expectations are deflated, the customer is resentful and unhappy, and returns the product.

Some times the pictures themselves are the problem. A smart phone manufacturer learned the hard way that there is more the packaging than selling the product. This particular cell phone manufacturer built it's latest phone with a lock to prevent activating the touch screen when the consumer was out an about doing their daily activities. To help sell and protect the smart phone, the manufacturer decided to put a plastic film over the touch screen and lock the phone.

The plastic film was a high definition picture of the actual home screen of the phone. You could look at the phone on the shelf in the store and see exactly what it would look like when you powered it up for the first time.

The phone was a marvel of innovative engineering. It was an instant hit upon arrival in the stores. Almost immediately, the company knew they had a problem. The return rate for the phone was over 35% in the first few weeks of sale. Further more, the no fault found rate was through the roof. Customers were returning non-defective phones at an alarming rate.

As it turned out, many of the returns were caused due to the phone being locked. The manufacturer did not bother to clarify this in their instructions or packaging.

Second, the high definition picture of the home screen was so realistic that many customers thought the phone was on and just would not work. They never pulled the film off the front of the phone so the touch screen would work.

Once these two issues were identified, the film as replaced with another protective film that clearly indicated that the protective cover should be removed and they stopped locking the phone at the factory.

Within days of selling the repackaged, slightly adjusted phones, the return rate fell right into place and their customers were bragging to everyone about their new, cool, smart phones. Unfortunately, there were probably many of the early buyers who bought a really cool smart phone from their competitor. They too probably went around bragging about their new phone, but they also probably trashed the maker of the original phone that, in their mind, was defective. As you can see, many times labeling and packaging is actually the cause of a return.

A red flag should arise is a product is repeatedly returned for reasons like: "item not as expected" or "not as advertised". Check labeling and packaging of the product. E-tailers should use the same diligence to ensure that product narratives and photos are an accurate representation of the product and its capabilities.

Here is a closing thought about reducing Internet returns. According to a comment posted on a survey by Dr. Mark Ferguson, items sold on the Internet that have customer reviews and comments, on average, have twenty percent fewer returns than similar items posted without customer reviews.

While there is no conclusive proof as to why this is the case, we believe that customer reviews provide more explanation to potential buyers about how items actually perform. A better informed consumer will be more likely to put more thought into the purchase and will be less likely to return the item once it has been purchased. The conclusion: e-tailers should utilize customer reviews as an active tool to lower return rates.

CHAPTER 14

Tax Treatment For Donating Returns

In the world of returns management, you often hear "we could donate this stuff and get more for it than we do when we process the returns and sell them on the secondary market."

While donating product to charity is altruistic and often results in charitable tax benefits, corporations that give to charity, generally, donate product for other reasons. While we are not tax experts, we do have extensive experience with Internal Revenue Service's (IRS) response to the charitable donation or returned goods. For companies that donate returns to charitable organizations, this chapter will outline the basics of receiving tax deductions for those donations.

The fact is most retailers and manufacturers do not take tax deductions for returned goods donated to charity. Many do give returned and damaged goods to charity, but few take a deduction for those donations. The primary reason is that there are established limits to the amount of charitable deduction a company may claim. Most companies reach that limit long before they determine the value of the returns that they have donated.

However, for the interested reader we have included an excerpt from the Federal Tax Code that covers donating product to charity. It is covered under Section 170e3 - Charitable, etc., contributions and gifts. This can be found on the web at www.law.cornell.edu/us-code/26/usc_sec_26_00000170----000-.html. We have provided a copy of the code as it appeared at the time this book was written.

Section 170e3 - Charitable, etc., contributions and gifts

(3) Special rule for certain contributions of inventory and other property

(A) Qualified contributions

For purposes of this paragraph, a qualified contribution shall mean a charitable contribution of property described in paragraph (1) or (2) of section 1221 (a), by a corporation (other than a corporation which is an S corporation) to an organization which is described in section 501 (c)(3) and is exempt under section 501 (a) (other than a private foundation, as defined in section 509 (a), which is not an operating foundation, as defined in section 4942 (j)(3)), but only if—

(i)   the use of the property by the donee is related to the purpose or function constituting the basis for its exemption under section 501 and the property is to be used by the donee solely for the care of the ill, the needy, or infants;

(ii)   the property is not transferred by the donee in exchange for money, other property, or services;

(iii)   the taxpayer receives from the donee a written statement representing that its use and disposition of the property will be in accordance with the provisions of clauses (i) and (ii); and

(iv) in the case where the property is subject to regulation under the Federal Food, Drug, and Cosmetic Act, as amended, such property must fully satisfy the applicable requirements of such Act and regulations promulgated thereunder on the date of transfer and for one hundred and eighty days prior thereto.

(B) Amount of reduction

The reduction under paragraph (1)(A) for any qualified contribution (as defined in subparagraph (A)) shall be no greater than the sum of—

(i) one-half of the amount computed under paragraph (1)(A) (computed without regard to this paragraph), and

(ii) the amount (if any) by which the charitable contribution deduction under this section for any qualified contribution (computed by taking into account the amount determined in clause (i), but without regard to this clause) exceeds twice the basis of such property.

(C) Special rule for contributions of food inventory

(i) General rule In the case of a charitable contribution of food from any trade or business of the taxpayer, this paragraph shall be applied—

(I) without regard to whether the contribution is made by a C corporation, and

(II) only to food that is apparently wholesome food.

(ii) Limitation In the case of a taxpayer other than a C corporation, the aggregate amount of such contributions for any taxable year which may be taken into account under this section shall not exceed 10 percent of the taxpayer's aggregate net income for such taxable year from all trades or businesses from which such contributions were made for such year, computed without regard to this section.

(iii) Apparently wholesome food For purposes of this subparagraph, the term "apparently wholesome food" has the meaning given to such term by section 22(b)(2) of the Bill Emerson Good Samaritan Food Donation Act (42 U.S.C. 1791 (b)(2)), as in effect on the date of the enactment of this subparagraph.

(iv) Termination This subparagraph shall not apply to contributions made after December 31, 2009.

(D) Special rule for contributions of book inventory to public schools

(i) Contributions of book inventory In determining whether a qualified book contribution is a qualified contribution, subparagraph (A) shall be applied without regard to whether the donee is an organization described in the matter preceding clause (i) of subparagraph (A).

(ii) Qualified book contribution For purposes of this paragraph, the term "qualified book contribution" means a charitable contribution of books to a public school which is an educational organization described in subsection (b)(1)(A)(ii) and which provides elementary education or secondary education (kindergarten through grade 12).

(iii) Certification by donee Subparagraph (A) shall not apply to any contribution of books unless (in addition to the certifications required by subparagraph (A) (as modified by this subparagraph)), the donee certifies in writing that—

(I) the books are suitable, in terms of currency, content, and quantity, for use in the donee's educational programs, and

(II) the donee will use the books in its educational programs.

(iv) Termination This subparagraph shall not apply to contributions made after December 31, 2009.

(E) This paragraph shall not apply to so much of the amount of the gain described in paragraph (1)(A) which would be long-term capital gain but for the application of sections 617, 1245, 1250, or 1252.

As with all things this complex, a qualified professional should be consulted before taking any action concerning any of the subjects listed above. Remember, tax law constantly change. Be sure to check with your company's internal tax accountant learn about any changes that may impact donating returns.

Good Samaritan Laws

Inside every company, there will be some that will argue against donating returned product or unsold consumable product to charity. They will argue that doing so could increase the risk of getting sued by a consumer who may be negatively affected by a charitable donation that originated in your company. A person becomes ill from a tainted can of green beans from the local food bank. Someone cuts his or her hand off with a chain saw given to Habitat for Humanity. Another gets struck by lightning while sleeping in a tent donated to the Boy Scouts.

Well, the good news is that people and organizations are protected when legitimately trying to help the less fortunate. The laws that provide this protection are referred to as Good Samaritan laws.

The Federal Good Samaritan Act was signed by President Clinton in 1996. It is referred to as the Bill Emerson Good Samaritan Food Donation Act. It was signed into law to encourage the donation of food and grocery products to non-profit charitable organizations for distribution to needy people.

The Federal Good Samaritan Act protects businesses, volunteers and non-profit organizations from civil or criminal liability in the course of donating apparently fit and wholesome food or grocery products for distribution to needy people. The Federal Good Samaritan Act is designed to encourage donations of food and grocery products by providing a uniform, national standard of liability for these types of donations.

This Act incorporated Title IV of the National and Community Service Act of 1990, from "model" legislation to permanent law, and transfers the Federal Good Samaritan Act to Section 22 of the Child Nutrition Act of 1966. The Federal Good Samaritan Act pre-empts various state Good Samaritan statutes with a single, federal standard of criminal and civil liability in the donation of food and grocery products.

However, many states have their own version of a Good Samaritan law that will offer additional protection over specific products and organizations. If you are concerned about donating specific goods to a charity, check with an attorney to see what protections are in place in your state.

From a federal standpoint, civil and criminal liability protection is extended to donors, persons, gleaners, and non-profit organizations arising from the nature, packaging, age, or condition of apparently wholesome food or apparently fit grocery products donated for distribution to needy people. There is some liability, however, but it is limited to acts of "gross negligence" or intentional misconduct, as defined by the Federal Good Samaritan Act. The bottom line is that, while donations to charity most likely will not eliminate your tax liability, it beats destroying the product. It will save landfill fees; natural resources; and the product will help those people who need it most. All in all, donating to charity is a better choice.

CHAPTER 15

Sustainability and Reverse Logistics

There is an approaching shortage in key, rare, earth minerals and metals used in the manufacturing of every major high tech piece of equipment. This natural resource depletion will likely alter the way products are manufactured and how reverse logistics programs dispose of them. It's happening faster than you might guess. The variety of natural resources are needed to manufacture PCs, TVs, smart phones, and routers will be depleted over the next ten to twenty-five years. According David Cohen's report, *Earth Audit*, our current consumption rate we will deplete the following rare, earth minerals by 2030 (page 38):

- Platinum
- Silver

- Indium
- Hafnium
- Antimony

Never heard of all these materials? Consumer electronics manufacturers know exactly what they are, and how to use them. The cost of these metals has already started to skyrocket and will clearly be one reason for consumer electronics price increases over the next twenty years.

Do you think that this warning sounds alarmist? This four-year-old data isn't relevant today because we are recycling more products, you muse. Not really. The same report found that many rare metals such as copper, zinc, and silver, have recycling rates of less than one third of the annual rate of consumption. (Page 35) For other metals, like platinum, we recycle less than one percent of annual consumption (page 35). To make the situation more difficult, the known reserves for many of the rare, earth metals are in countries such as China and Kazakhstan, where the availability of these materials is far from guaranteed.

In fact, in 2010, according to the June issue of National Geographic, China supplied 97% of the worlds rare earth minerals. It was noted that China and Japan got into a diplomatic dispute with one another and China stopped all exports of rare earth minerals to them until the dispute was resolved.

All of this will force significantly more re-manufacturing and re-cycling. This will drive the need for and importance of world-class reverse logistics. **Most importantly, we believe that, within the next ten years, reverse logistics will become the most important part of a manufacturer's supply chain.**

Today's design and manufacturing processes will, by necessity, change dramatically and designers will have to build remanufacturing concepts into the original design specifications. These same manufacturers will rely on a sophisticated, cost-effective reverse logistics process that will provide the majority of materials needed to re-manufacture new product for their primary market.

Today, many manufacturers ignore returned assets. They may recycle some of the easy-to-retrieve metals and components but, for the most part, manufacturers write-off the value of old components. Every new unit manufactured is made from newly acquired resources. Production costs, driven by significant shortages, will change these methods and require sophisticated reverse logistics programs to fuel additional manufacturing.

Because manufacturers have ignored the value of the end-of -life products, the secondary market buyer has seized the opportunity to capture the value of this inventory. It is estimated that at least forty-five percent of all returned consumer electronics will be resold on the secondary market. We participated in a study completed by Dr. Dale Rogers, while at the University of Nevada Reno, that examined the secondary market. This market has grown significantly over the last twenty years and is now estimated to make up 2.24% of US GDP, according to a study conducted by Dr. Dale Rogers and his team, one of which was co-author Curtis Greve.

This clearly demonstrates the value of returned and end-of-life products. In the future, consumer electronics manufacturers will be forced to recapture the value of goods currently flowing through the secondary market, as the cost of metals and rare, earth minerals escalate.

When this occurs, it will be a truly sustainable supply chain. The reality is, for most corporations today, sustainability is really nothing more than selling scrap for a few pennies or recycling corrugated. This will change.

Where Did Sustainability Come From?

Where did the concept of sustainability originate? In 2004, Dr. Dale S. Rogers, suggested that logistics professionals work together to develop a sustainable supply chain model that focuses on complete product life-cycle management and develop what he called "sustainability". Dr. Rogers envisioned a revolution in the logistics industry that is now upon us.

Today, sustainability initiatives are everywhere. Over eighty percent of the Global 1000 companies issue a separate sustainability report to stockholders. (8) Every manufacturer of consumer goods, in large part thanks to Walmart, has made major strides to incorporate sustainability programs into their manufacturing and logistics process. You can listen to a series of podcasts entitled: *Sustainable Supply Chain Management* at www.grevedavis.com to learn more on the topic. (16)

In our eco-conscious world, virtually every company highlights its sustainability efforts. It is clear that there is a concerted effort to develop sustainability throughout the corporate world. However, many of these companies often commit one of the *Six Sins of Greenwashing*, (17) which is simply declaring themselves environmentally friendly without changing any behaviors or outcomes, An often-confusing and overlooked piece of the sustainability puzzle is end-of-life" product management, which is determined by the organization's reverse logistics capabilities.

Factoring end-of-life strategies into product manufacturing is the key to making products truly sustainable and maximizing the long-term value of those products. Reverse Logistics provides the infrastructure to realize the true value of assets that are at the end of their usable life. The reverse logistics process completes the full loop of product life cycle management and should always indicate the highest and best use of a product.

Sustainability Teams Often Ignore Reverse Logistics

Recently I gave a presentation at a conference on reverse logistics and asked roughly three hundred reverse logistics executives in attendance three questions about sustainability within their organization and received these responses:

1. How many of you work for companies that have ongoing sustainability initiatives? Everyone raised his or her hands.
2. How many of you work for companies that have a cross-functional team working to develop sustainability initiatives? Again, hands filled the air.
3. How many of you sit on that cross-functional, sustainability team within your organization? Only TWO people raised their hands.

Companies that are serious about developing sustainable practices must incorporate reverse logistics into their efforts or those efforts will be incomplete, ineffective and more costly. Reverse logistics adds value to sustainability efforts in three major ways.

Provides the infrastructure to remove outdated, obsolete, re-called, and defective assets from the primary stream of commerce. Uses existing systems to provide a disposition for those assets in an alternative stream of commerce such as liquidation; repair; refurbishment; recycling; parts or metal harvesting; or disposal.

Processes inventory and other material in an affordable, controllable, and visible manner that will reduce the total cost of processing returns and greatly reduce legal risk.

Extends the life of assets by re-manufacturing, repairing, reselling, or recycling goods that flow through the reverse logistics pipeline.

While sustainability has many facets, at the end of the day, it is always about eliminating waste. A reverse logistics program is at the end of the supply chain where assets are either repurposed or destroyed. If your organization does not have a reverse logistics process or if the reverse logistics team is left out of sustainability strategy sessions, you have an opportunity to dramatically improve your overall sustainability results.

In the future, reverse logistics executives will not only need to have a seat at the sustainability table, they will be a critical member of the design, manufacturing, and customer satisfaction team for many companies.

CHAPTER 16

The Future of Reverse Logistics

When writing this book, gas prices were at $3.99 per gallon. Diesel was slightly higher but nobody can really explain why. Fuel prices have never been higher in the U.S. We point this out because fuel prices are expected to double during the next three to five years. When eventuality becomes reality, and there is hardly anyone that doubts that it will, the existing reverse supply chain networks will not be economically sound. In fact, many existing forward distribution networks will not be as economically efficient as they should be either.

The rising costs of transportation combined with facility fixed costs will force executives to redesign the reverse logistics networks in order to minimize their total cost of processing returns. The number and size of a nationwide facility network is designed around these two important variables: transportation costs and fixed warehouse expenses.

Current reverse logistics networks are all designed based on transportation costs that used two dollars, or less, per gallon fuel prices. In 2008, when diesel prices were over $4.25 per gallon---and actually went above five dollars per gallon in some locations---existing reverse logistics networks were costing much more to operate than the value of the inventory being processed.

For example, there are a number of retail chains that were shipping ten-dollar clock radios from the west coast to the east coast, and then selling them on the secondary market for $1.50 to a salvage buyer in Florida. The cost of processing and transportation for so little return made no sense. Soon items like this were being thrown in the dumpster or donated to a local charity.

Visibility was lost, execution was sporadic, and the only thing that saved many companies from greater regulatory liabilities and fraudulent returns was the quick drop in fuel prices. As quickly as fuel spiked, it dropped back down in the fall. Everyone acted like the spike in fuel prices was a bad dream and, upon awakening, went back to business as usual.

The Regulators Are Here

The potential for disaster has grown ominously large and looms over the industry. Since 2008, thirty-five states have passed regulations that increase the potential liability for improperly disposing of consumer products. Many major retailers have been hit with hefty fines. Smart companies are developing store-level procedures to ensure that returned and recalled products are processed according to strict policies. All to avoid future fines, bad press and penalties.

Manufacturers have felt the regulatory pain as well. They have had to develop their own guidelines for processing returns that mirror their customers---retailers---guidelines. The story is the same for industrial sectors as it is for consumer products. The regulatory landscape has become muddled and unnavigable. So much so, that the Consumer Electronics Association has lobbied Congress to pass a federal law that will supersede various state regulations concerning processing end-of-life goods; and provide one set of regulations uniformly across the country.

On the surface, this move may appear to be inviting the fox for a sleepover in the henhouse. But, it is apparent that, without some form of federal regulation, retailers and manufacturers will be left alone to deal with the regulations promulgated by fifty different state legislative bodies. Regulatory variations and requirements will be difficult, if not impossible, to keep abreast of and follow. The attendant costs to this process will certainly be high. The unknown risks will be greater and, taken together with the cost of compliance, will have a dramatic impact on the share price of every manufacturer and retailer in the United States.

That being said, no one company has taken serious steps to redesign their networks to minimize the impact of rising fuel prices and mitigate the risks associated with increased legislation that is impacts returns and recalled products. While most companies are taking a "We will believe it when we see it position", we believe that, over the next twenty years, every viable company will be forced to redesign their reverse logistics network due to the inexorable increase in the price of energy.

Internet Sales Increase Return Volumes

In addition, Internet sales continue to command a larger share of total retail and business-to-business sales. For many product categories, Internet sales return rates can be three to five times higher than traditional brick and mortal return rates. Primarily, because the consumer cannot touch and feel the product when ordering it on line. You cannot tell if a picture of a blue curtain will really match your blue pillowcase until you get it home. On-line buyers also tend to return more product simply because they have changed their minds between the time they bought the item on line and the time it was delivered to their home.

However, there are some best practices that can be used to reduce Internet return rates. For example, according to Dr. Mark Ferguson of the Georgia Institute of Technology, items sold on the Internet that have associated customer reviews have a twenty percent lower return rate than those items that do not have customer reviews. Furthermore, return rates for items that have fifty or more reviews are seventy-five percent lower than items without any reviews. (18) This is a striking, compelling piece of information that should help e-tailers reduce return rates and, subsequently, the total cost of returns.

Companies such as Home Shopping Network (HSN) track customer returns using a sophisticated system that identifies trends such as customers who always return clothing from size six but keep size eight. Home Shopping Network provides this information to their call center that, in turn, communicates with the customer to attempt to avoid a return. This information also and more importantly, ensures that the customer is happy with their purchase and HSNs service.

So what does the future hold for reverse logistics? More volume, more costs, and more liability? For some, this will be the case. Those companies that embrace the need for change and redesign their reverse logistics network, will actually have a network in place that will cost less to process higher volumes while minimizing potential liability.

How? We believe the reverse logistics network of the future will be a decentralized processing model with centralized control and visibility. Over the last twenty years, reverse logistics has gotten significantly more sophisticated and information capable.

It is not unusual for a manufacturer to purchase reverse logistics software from one software provider; outsource return center operations to another provider who performs gate keeping and reconciliation functions; and subcontract repair and refurbishing services to a product repair specialist. In addition, some manufacturers hire a liquidator to sell their goods on the domestic or international secondary markets.

A Typical Reverse Logistics Network

Adding transportation management, recycling, parts harvesting, metal reclamation, and waste management to the reverse logistics management package results in an interrelated network of at least seven companies that unite to provide a working reverse logistics network for the one prototypical company.

If your company is global and manufacturers a wide variety of items, your reverse logistics network could easily encompass sixteen, twenty-four or even thirty or more organizations. Each organization has a specific function that only it provides. Each one has its own, unique contract with a unique set of terms, conditions, and incentives.

As indicated in the chart below, tomorrow's reverse logistics network is far from simple. This complex, interdependent network must be closely monitored and requires a full-time staff of executives to ensure that it is operated efficiently and effectively.

Reverse Logistics Network of Service Providers

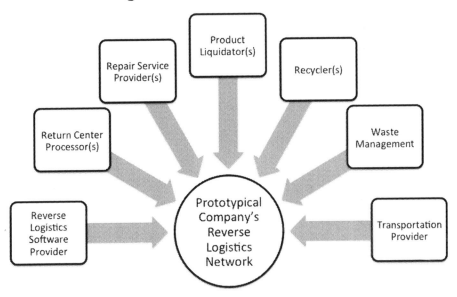

Redesigning Your Reverse Logistics Network

For the purposes of this book, the future of reverse logistics is defined as the next three to five years. We believe that, between the time this book is published in 2011, and 2015, rising fuel costs will force virtually every company to rethink their reverse logistics networks. Couple this with the predicted rare, earth mineral and metal shortages and you can clearly see how much things will have to change in order to survive the future.

These redesigned networks must include much more than simply creating other facilities and functions just like the old ones. New processes will be needed, improved visibility will be needed, and new partners will be required around the globe.

The ramifications of this paradigm shift are significant. Following, is a compilation of possibilities that will shape reverse logistics network of tomorrow.

- Sophisticated software that will allow regional or local processing with centralized visibility.

- Many more regional processing centers, much smaller than the existing facilities or co-located with other companies. Not simply increasing from one facility to two. According to Dr. Dale Rogers, the cost-effective network will consist of eight, ten or even fifteen facilities. (11)

- Small, regionalized sub-networks of repair service providers, facility operators, recyclers, and waste management companies will be centered on a regional processing center or located within the regional processing facilities themselves. All efficiently integrated and centrally managed.

- Service providers within your network will be more specialized. Today you might have one repair vendor that repairs PCs. Tomorrow you may have three on each coast for PCs, plus one on each coast for TVs and monitors. A half of a dozen small mechanical repair shops, a couple of parts harvesters and four or five specialized recyclers would round out your service provider network.

- Outsourcing to a single, third-party reverse logistics provider who is responsible for all reverse logistics functions, give ways to a mixed network of best-in-class providers that are cheaper, more efficient, and have a lower cost of change, thus lowering the risk of outsourcing.

- Product at lower price points will be liquidated locally or donated to charity to avoid disposal costs and related liabilities.
- Point-of-sale systems will be integrated with reverse logistics management systems to provide a holistic view of the reverse logistics pipeline. These consolidated reports provide product returns information, recovery rates, item disposition totals, sustainability reports, and regulatory compliance reports.
- Recycling will dramatically increase as many of the rare, earth minerals are exhausted and remanufacturing grows.
- Retailers will push suppliers to take product back and pay transportation expenses or pay for product disposal and losses on recycling.
- Manufacturers will sell product returns on the secondary market directly from the retailers return centers, thus avoiding one leg of transportation and processing costs.
- "B" retailers will flourish.
- The secondary market will experience a significant consolidation with a handful of major liquidators controlling the majority of the secondary sales. These companies will be sophisticated brokers with global, multi-channel capabilities.
- Virtually nothing will be thrown into a landfill. The only waste will be hazardous material that will be incinerated or disposed of in a hazardous material dumpsite.
- Internet sales will continue to grow and they will experience continually rising return rates.
- Increasing costs of rare, earth minerals and other inflationary factors in the market will force manufacturers to begin developing re-manufacturing programs that will make up an ever-growing piece of their primary, first-line production.
- Products will be manufactured with end-of-life in mind.

All of these factors will increase the importance and visibility of reverse logistics within every organization. As a result, executives responsible for reverse logistics will not only have access to his company's senior team, he will have a seat at the table and assume a key role between manufacturing, sales, and supply chain functions.

In chapter to follow, we will discuss the coming evolution in manufacturing processes that will make reverse logistics the most complex and important part of a manufacturer's supply chain. The driver behind this is a set of factors that is referred to as **servicizing.**

CHAPTER 17

Servicizing – Product

Life Cycle Extension

I n their white paper, *"Servicizing: The Quiet Transition to Extended Product Responsibility,"* authors White, Stoughton and Feng provide the following definition of servicizing:

The emergence of product-based services which blur the distinction between manufacturing and traditional service sector activities. (Page 2)

Reverse logistics will undergo more change during the next ten years than it has during the last fifty. The industry will become much more sophisticated and will take on a significantly more prominent role within the supply chain. Much of this change will be caused by the adoption of remanufacturing processes, the concept of which is "servicizing."

Servicizing is an odd sounding term that evokes images of fast food and large orders of fries but it is far from that. Servicizing is actually the development of a product's life cycle to incorporate customer returns, testing, repair, refurbishment, recycling, and re-manufacturing into the product's initial development plan. By incorporating the principles learned from reverse logistics into new product development, manufacturers can reduce their dependence upon the critical, and increasingly scarce, resources used in the traditional manufacturing process by reusing a significant number of the resources already included in previous newly-manufactured units.

This process is that we call The Product Life Cycle Extension Loop©. For companies to effectively adopt this idea, a critical shift in thinking must take place at every level within the organization's product development team.

Changing Mindset Is The Key

The key here is to change one's perspective on how new products are produced. Servicizing may not be the complete answer for every manufacturer. However, for products containing rare, earth minerals, or products whose core components' useful life is significantly greater than the life of the whole unit, designing Servicizing concepts into the production plan will dramatically reduce the total cost of producing new products over the long haul. Servicizing will reduce the dependence on raw materials, and risks from hazardous material disposal.

The Product Life Cycle Extension Loop©

Today's manufacturing process will have to change in order to do this. Manufacturers will have to incorporate the Product Life Cycle Extension Loop© in order to realize the benefits from Servicizing. The Life Cycle Extension Loop© is illustrated in the following diagram:

The Product Lifecycle Extension Loop©

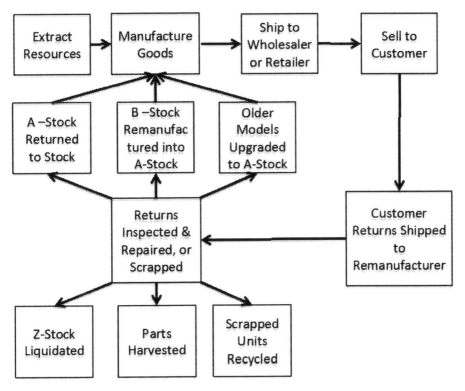

Rising Costs of Resources – The Driver Behind Servicizing

Depending on a manufacturer's existing production facilities and reverse logistics processes, the investment required to build the infrastructure for a Product Life Cycle Extension Loop© can be significant. In the long run, however, these costs will be minimal compared to the potential costs of raw materials over the near term.

Everyone is aware of the rising cost of oil and oil by-products. In previous chapters we pointed out that fuel prices are expected to increase by fifty percent or more over the next five years. This increase will pale in comparison to the rising costs of rare, earth minerals, many of which you probably have never heard of before.

Rare earth minerals are used in the production of a plethora of consumer goods---food and clothing. Metals such as platinum zinc, indium, and gallium are used in the production of cell phones, flat screen monitors, big screen TVs, and just about all of the electronic gadgets currently being sold. The known reserves of these resources will be depleted as early as 2020, according to Cohen's article, *Earth Audit*. (Page 38)

Prices for these metals have increased dramatically since 2005 and their rate of inflation will only go higher until humans exhaust the supply of these rare, earth minerals all together.

According to Cohen, there remains the following supply of these rare, earth minerals: (page number)

Mineral	Approximate Remaining Supply (In Years)
Indium	10
Hafnium	10
Platinum	15
Silver	20
Tantalum	40
Uranium	40
Zinc	40

Will we exhaust our supply of all of these metals over the next four decades? Probably not completely, but you can be assured that the prices for every one of them will explode as supply is depleted. These rare, earth metals will see hyperinflation that will rival anything in recorded financial history.

Additionally, the known reserves for many of these rare, earth minerals are not in the most politically-friendly or easily-accessed locations on the planet. Locations such as the Amazon Basin, Kazakhstan, central Australia, South Africa, and central China have the largest, and in some cases, only known reserves of rare, earth metals. The economies in these locations will see a boom as the value of their local mining industry dramatically increases. The impact on the rest of us will be much different. Our costs rise sharply.

Some believe that substitute minerals will be found or that man-made alternatives developed, if those predictions are accurate, some of the shortfall will be filled. However, it is unlikely that a significant number of rare, earth minerals and listed above will have a suitable replacement discovered or developed. The resulting shortages will cause skyrocketing inflation that will ripple through every facet of the global economy.

The reality of this situation has already impacted on our financial markets. The price of silver had significant growth in 2010. In March 2010, CNBC * staged a roundtable discussion to discover why. The conclusion: the dramatic increase in the price of silver was partially due to a weak global economy. However, the larger driver in the high price of silver was the continued and growing demand by manufacturers. One of the guests described silver as the canary in the coal mine when it comes to rare, earth metals.

Inflated Mineral Costs Will Drive Servicizing

The major impact of hyper inflated rare, earth mineral prices on manufacturers and their customers, will be the need to develop alternatives to traditional product development methods. They will be forced to develop a Product Life Cycle Extension Loop©.

Today, there are a number of industries that rely on a Product Life Cycle Extension Loop©. Many consumers rely on them as well, and are not even aware of it.

The Cable Set Top Box Repair Industry – An Example

The best example is the Cable Set Top Box business. Today, in homes all across the world, people are watching their favorite television shows thanks to their cable set top box. In the old days, a cable came out of the wall and the homeowner would connect it directly to the back of the TV.

Today, the cable company sends a technician to a home with a set top box under his arm. Typically, consumers don't know who manufactured their set top box, and don't really care as long as American Idol or Dancing with the Stars comes in crystal clear.

On the front of the set top box, there is number of plug-ins and slots for components. The consumer doesn't care if it is brand new or if it has been refurbished or rebuilt. It works and the customer is happy.

What most people do not know is that eighty-five percent of the set top boxes newly installed in homes are not new at all. In fact, the majority of set top boxes is repaired and/or refurbished. The unused slots and plug-ins on the front of the unit are designed into the frame in the event they are needed for future enhancements.

When the unit breaks or is upgraded by the customer, either the repair technician personally swap the old one for a new one, or the cable company will mail the customer a replacement unit with instructions to return the old unit.

The returned unit is sent to the cable company's return center where the returned set top box is tested, inspected, repaired, refurbished, repackaged, and put back into sellable stock.

The total cost of processing the returned unit through the reverse logistics pipeline and back into stock is less than half of the cost of buying a new set top box. (14) Cable providers have developed a system that keeps their product acquisition cost low while keeping their customer satisfaction high.

The only projected change in this model over the next twenty years is that many cable companies plan to simplify the setup function so that fewer technicians are needed for home installation.

We believe, that in the future, this model will make sense for many other items, especially high-value electronics and items that undergo constant improvement or enhanced technology. We also believe that there will be an opportunity for retailers to develop unique programs that will provide the latest equipment with the most up to date features to their customers for less money, while recognizing the need to conserve the rare, earth minerals and metals.

Servicizing Will Present Opportunities

How much would it be worth to a retailer to have a ten-year lease on a big screen TV with a customer, that included free technology upgrades and/or replacement every three to five years? Programs of this nature eliminate purchasing risks and provide the customer assurance that they will be abreast of continual advancement in technology which currently, forces the purchase new equipment before their existing equipment comes to end-of-life,

Retailers secure guaranteed customer for the term of the lease, as well as the potential retail benefit of that customer purchasing related equipment and accessories. Smart retailers will offer a lease-renewal program each time the customer upgrades to newer technology. Would you take advantage of a program like this? This is simply a variation of the programs that AT&T* and Verizon have developed to encourage loyalty to their brand. Many people stick with their carrier because of a long-term contract, affordable upgrades, and warranty programs.

Today, manufacturers or resellers of cell phones and cable set top boxes are, in fact, providing Product Life Cycle Extension Programs©. In the future, manufacturers practically every high-value product that requires rare, earth minerals will find an economic imperative to offer a similar program.

Today, most companies recycle to avoid liability and difficulties with regulators. Tomorrow, they will have enhanced recycling programs because it will put money on the bottom line.

Today, many manufacturers repair and refurbish returned products but they liquidate the resulting units on the secondary market. They do this to get some return on the repaired assets and to avoid end-of-life liability.

Tomorrow, many manufacturers will incorporate reverse logistics processes into their design and build functions to control costs, avoid risks associated with supplies of rare earth metals and provide consumers with the products they want at prices they can afford. Like the major airlines, do today, they will realize significant bottom line contributions from dramatically extending the Life Cycle of the primary unit produced as a result of "servicizing their processes, and avoiding having to pay hyper inflated costs for new raw materials.

CHAPTER 18

What Manufacturers Can Do To Reduce Returns

When a manufacturer meets with their customers to discuss the selling of product, often the subject of returns comes up. The management of customer returns is as much a part of selling most products as the marketing program or package design. The methods that can be used to reduce the number of customer returns are less often discussed than the policies and procedures used to govern them. This is unfortunate because the best way to reduce the cost of returns and the eventual impact on a products margin is to reduce the number of items that customers bring back.

While this appears overly simplified, the fact is that only 20% of products returned are actually defective. The opportunity for every manufacturer is to take proactive steps to reduce the other 80% of returns that are not defective. If this can be done, the impact on profits and customer satisfaction can be significant.

These proactive steps can be accomplished by educating your primary customer, providing understandable instructions, and a common sense approach to meeting the needs of consumers after the sale. The practice of producing ever more strict returns policies will only turn off customers and, in the end, reduce sales. As mentioned previously in this book, restricting customer return privileges have historically done more to restrict sales than to restrict returns.

Many manufacturers often find themselves in situations where they rely on distributors, sales people, retailers, or other middlemen to deal with the customer and their returns. However, there are a number of things that a manufacturer can do to increase their ultimate customer's satisfaction with the product and prevent the return.

Let's look at a few ways that a manufacturer can help minimize the chances of a customer becoming dissatisfied with their product and returning their product.

The first step a manufacturer should take to reduce returns is to carefully look at the packaging of the item. Packaging serves three purposes. The first purpose is to protect the item while is working it's way into the hands of the consumer. The second purpose is to help sell the item to the consumer. The third, and often overlooked purpose of packaging is to establish the consumer's expectations of the product and educate them on the product's use.

Companies will spend millions on packaging design but never think about how this design could actually drive customer returns. When looking at the packaging, view it through the eyes of your customer, not the marketing department or the design engineer. The art on the packaging, along with the instructions should provide multiple angles of the product and be thought of as the first step in establishing the customer's expectation of the product. If assembly is required, progressive stages of the product should guide the customer through the assembly process. Look at how your product is packaged as your first line of defense against returns and your first opportunity to educate the consumer about your product.

Instructions and package inserts, like the external packaging, will also impact product return rates and customer satisfaction. Instructions must be clear, concise, accurate and easy to understand. Most importantly, they must be written in the voice of the customer, using terms they understand and avoiding industry jargon that will only cause frustration and confusion. Do not leave the responsibility of developing the instruction to your product engineers alone. They should be reviewed and edited by a cross section of people within your organization. This should include customer focus groups, executive assistance, spouses, warehouse worker and even an executive.

You can feel confident that product returns will be minimized if a good representative team has reviewed the instructions and successfully used the instruction to assemble the product.

For goods with components, such as consumer electronic products, be certain that all the connectors, wires, outlets, and ends are color-coded and that the wires are bundled together in logical kits. If it is possible to label parts or wires with a letter or number, by all means do so. Regular folks find that to be of great assistance in assembling a product. Note those facts in the instruction manual.

In addition, whether your products are sold around the world or only in English speaking countries, print all instructions and inserts should in multiple languages. The voice of many customers is not speaking English. The easier it is for them to read the instructions, the better.

For many products, it is important for the customer to take specific steps first in order for the item to work properly. A good example of this is wireless phone that should be plugged in for twenty four hours prior to using it for the first time, or a smart phone that has a clear protect cover on the phone that has to be removed in order for the touch screen to work. If not brought to the customer's attention, the item will appear to be defective and will be returned by many.

A best practice to address this is what we call "Stop Sheets". These are brightly colored inserts that are packaged with the product that will have one or two messages in large font. We call them "Stop Sheets" because they often have a big stop sign on them or they scream "STOP" at the customer. Use "Stop Sheets" to call attention to the one or two mistakes they make that cause returns because of user error. Many times these brightly colored inserts instruct consumers to call your 1-800 technical support line before returning the product.

Many manufacturers have 800 technical support lines to address customer issues which prevent needless returns. These number should be on all instructions and box inserts that are available to the consumer. Do not hide the number or make it difficult for the customer to find. Customer support numbers should be in large, clear fonts and could specify that customers must call the technical support line before returning the item. The support line should be staffed when your customers are most likely to need it. That means evenings and weekends if selling products to everyday consumers. This is the time when most of your customers will be assembling your products. It is always amazing to find see a consumer product support line open from 9:00am to 4:30 pm, Monday thru Friday.

If you have a support line, call it a on a regular basis and see how you are treated. Were they accessible when your customer needs them? How long were you on hold? Did they provide the service in a manner that reflects positively on your organization? How your customers are treated when they call your technical support lines will dictate how they think of your company for years to come.

Years ago there were a number of studies that found that if customers were upset they would tell, on average nine other people. Well, that is not true anymore. Today, an upset customer will tell nine other people, PLUS they will tweet about it, update their Facebook page, post it on Linked In, blog about it, test a dozen of their friends and send out a few emails just to make a point. Today, if you make one customer made, thousands hear about it instantly and it will be in cyberspace for years to come.

To summarize, many manufacturers are unknowingly causing returns and creating customer dissatisfaction because of a lot of reasons that really have nothing to do with their product. To reduce your customer's rate of returns look beyond the product. Spend time looking at the "non-verbal" signals you are giving your customer. Consider your aftersales support processes. Ask yourself if you are actually creating returns because of these factors. You will quickly see that making effective use of your packaging, instructions, inserts and 1-800 tech support lines are cost effective methods to improve customers satisfaction and reducing product returns.

CHAPTER 19

101 Things You Always Wanted to Know About Reverse Logistics

The following list of 101 things you always wanted to know about reverse logistics is based on our forty plus years of experience working in reverse logistics, our personal opinions, battle scars and even some published information.

1. A company's customer returns policy limits the risk of their customers when making a purchase, thus is the company's guarantee of satisfaction to their customer. It can be a prime sales driver or a sales inhibitor.

2. There are basically two types of returns: customer returns and recalls.

3. Only about twenty percent of customer returns are actually functionally defective.

4. Half of all consumer returns are sent to the original manufacturer who will either destroy them, recycle them, re-manufacturer them, or sell them on the secondary market.

5. There are only six things you can do with any returned item. You can return it to the OEM, put it back in stock, sell it on the secondary market, donate it to charity, recycle it, or throw it away.

6. Roughly, half of all returns are sold on the secondary market.

7. Approximately forty percent of all returns sold on the secondary market are exported outside of the United States.

8. The United States secondary market is estimated to be 2.25% of U.S. GDP. (4)

9. U.S. consumers return more every year, than the total GDP of sixty-six percent of the nations in the world. (2) That makes U.S. consumer returns larger than the size of the economy of Turkey!

10. The consumer product safety commission has issued over four hundred recalls in each of the last two years.

11. The FDA has ordered over two hundred different pharmaceutical recalls from the market every year for the past ten years.

12. It is estimated that, for every mandatory pharmaceutical recall issued by the FDA, there is one voluntary recall issued by the manufacturer. The vast majority of all recalls are for errors in packaging, instructions, or other reasons that pose no health threat to the public.

13. The majority of big-box retailers have one or more return centers strategically located based on population density, transportation costs, and fixed warehouse costs.

14. Smaller format stores, such as small mall shops, send returns directly from the store to the manufacturer or distributor.

15. The average return rate for all retailers, according to the NRF, is 8.1% of sales.(5)

16. The average return rate for automotive retailers is three percent.

17. The average return rate for big box retailers is six percent.

18. The average return rate for department stores can range from fifteen to thirty percent of sales depending upon the season.

19. The average pharmaceutical manufacturer's return rate is two percent of annual sales.

20. Pharmaceutical recalls account for eighty percent of all pharmaceutical returns.

21. Over seventy percent of non-recall related pharmaceutical returns are due to reaching the date of expiration or are to short dated to sell.

22. Products sold on line that have easily accessible customer reviews have a twenty percent lower rate of return compared to other similar products that do not have customer reviews or comments. (18)

23. Return rates for items sold on line that have fifty or more reviews have a return rate that is seventy-five percent less than similar products that do not have customer reviews or comments.

24. Return rates for consumer electronics in the U.S. ranges between eleven and twenty percent of sales.

25. Return rates for consumer electronics in Europe range between two and nine percent of sales

26. On average, at least forty percent of consumer electronics returns are not defective. (8)

27. The busiest time of year for big-screen TV returns is the week following the Super Bowl.

28. Delays in processing electronics returns will reduce recovery values, on average, by ten percent, per month delayed.

29. The busiest month for camcorder returns is July, after the honeymoons are over.

30. According to the HDMA, pharmaceutical returns and recalls cost manufacturers approximately $5.8 billion every year.

31. Returns cost manufacturers in the U.S. between nine and fourteen percent of sales every year. (6)

32. Liberal return policies actually reduce the overall percentage of returns to sales over time.

33. Restrictive return policies have reduced sales by a wider margin than they reduce returns, thus increasing the percent of sales returned.

34. If a U.S. consumer's returns experience is positive, they will return to shop again eighty-five percent of the time, whether they received a refund or not. (11)

35. If the returns experience is negative, ninety-five percent of U.S. consumers surveyed said they would NOT return to shop, even if they did receive a full refund for the original return. (11)

36. The average recovery rate for general merchandise retailers selling product on the secondary market averages around fifteen percent of costs.

37. "As is" consumer electronics sold on the secondary market, on average, recover approximately twenty-five percent of the original cost of the item.

38. Repaired electronics sold on the secondary market to bulk buyers will fetch between forty-five and sixty percent of original cost, depending on the item and the season.

39. Repaired electronics sold directly to a consumer, with a warranty, can be sold up to ninety percent of regular retail for a like item.

40. Many repair service providers claim they complete a DoD wipe of all hard drives returned. This means the hard drives have been reformatted at least seven times.

41. Secondary market buyers will sell product on commission for a fee that ranges between seven and twenty percent depending on the item and the market.

42. The yield rate of a typical high tech repair facility will be between ninety-five and ninety-eight percent of all units tested.

43. The scrap rate for a typical high tech repair facility will be between three and five percent of total units received.

44. Less than fifteen percent of parts used in high tech repair facilities that service big-box retailers are purchased new.

45. The majority of parts used in repair facility are taken from other non-repairable units.

46. Major retailers that liquidate their returns sell on average seventy-five percent of those returns to bulk buyers.

47. Only less than ten percent of returns liquidated on the secondary market are sold directly to consumers.

48. Peak season for consumer returns begins the second week of January through the second week of March.

49. Peak season for general merchandise retailers can account for up to forty-five percent of total returns processed.

50. Peak season for Internet retailers can account for up to eighty percent of total returns processed.

51. Approximately seventy percent of all fragrances sold have been previously returned, repackaged and re-stocked for re-sale in the primary sales channels.

52. The cost of processing, testing, and repackaging fragrances is less than twenty percent of the cost of manufacturing a new bottle of the same fragrance.

53. The average off-invoice allowance for grocery returns is less than two percent of total sales.

54. The majority of grocery returns are donated to food banks, farms, and dog pounds.

55. Over eighty percent of all set top boxes put into new homes by cable companies are repaired or refurbished equipment.

56. Most cell phones, set top boxes, and game consoles in North America are sent to Mexico when they are required to be repaired or refurbished.

57. The cost of a repair technician in the U.S..is five times greater than the cost of a repair technician in Mexico.

58. Less than one percent of goods and packaging processed through a return center is thrown into a landfill or is incinerated.

59.   The standard measurement for through-put in a return facility is total variable hours divided by total units received.

60.   The average through-put for a big-box retailer's return center will range between eighty to 110 units per hour.

61.   Revenue from recycling typically goes to the company who has ownership of the product being recycled.

62.   3PLs that recycle product normally are paid based on their normal labor rates for processing product, as opposed to sharing the recycling revenue.

63.   Many recyclers of plastic, cardboard, and other materials will provide bailers, pre-crushers, and other equipment at no or substantially reduced cost in order to get the recycled materials for free or a lower cost.

64.   On average, it is thirty percent more cost effective to recycle K resin A plastic hangers than it is to buy new hangers.

65.   The average through-put for a grocery reclamation center will range between 300 and 500 units per hour. (cite)

66.   The biggest challenges in operating a food reclamation center are pests and odor control.

67.   The average repair technician should be able to repair six to ten units per hour, depending on the unit and testing requirements.

68.   The average return center will turn inventory eighteen to twenty-six times per year, depending on the product lines being processed.

69.   The average returns center has less than 0.02% shrinkage.

70.   The majority of major retailers outsource return center operations to 3PLs.

71.   The typical contract for an outsourced return center, other than a high tech repair facility, is a cost-plus contract with a budget cap.

72.   The typical high tech return center contract is based on a cost-per-unit-repaired.

73. The average management fee for 3PLs operating return centers range between twelve and eighteen percent of total operating costs. Some will have fees in the four to six percent range if they are able to liquidate the product that is not being returned to the manufacturer.

74. There are over thirty different reverse logistics software providers in the U.S. and in Europe.

75. Reverse logistics software is sold either as a site license or charged on a cost-per-unit basis.

76. The average site license for a retailer's reverse logistics software package will range between $150,000 per facility up to $500,000 per facility.

77. The average site licenses for a manufacturer's reverse logistics software package will range between $75,000 per facility up to $300,000 per facility

78. Maintenance expenses for reverse logistics management systems are typically fifteen percent of the cost of the site license or its equivalent.

79. The majority or reverse logistics systems receive uploads and downloads from the customers various systems using flat file feeds.

80. Customer returns accounts for the largest influx of inventory that will be used to fill orders for catalog and Internet retailers.

81. The largest category of returns for repair shops is "Ordered too Many." This accounts for thirty percent of all returns.

82. The biggest cause of a consumer's returned purchases is some from of buyer's remorse.

83. The biggest reason shops in the field return parts or orders is because the customer cancelled the job.

84. Retailers will charge vendors consolidation fees ranging from one percent of the cost of the product up to ten percent. The average for most retailers is around 3.5%

85. Retailer consolidation fees charged to manufacturers offset the cost of consolidating individual store returns centrally and

transportation costs from the store to the centralized returns processing facility.

86.   Large electronics manufacturers rarely agree to consolidation fees, even with the largest retailers, because they can get away with it.

87.   The majority of the time, manufacturers pay transportation costs from a retailer's return center to manufacturer's return facility.

88.   There are three types of return authorizations manufacturers generally give retailers; Call for RA, Standing RA, No RA Required.

89.   Many retailers will forego consolidation fees in negotiations to get either a Standing RA or No RA Required.

90.   Re-returns are shipments of returned goods that have been shipped to a manufacturer and were shipped back to the retailer because of some violation in return preparation or return agreement.

91.   Sorted goods that are shipped back to the vendor or sold on the secondary market are generally segregated into shipping units either by dollar value of the shipment, quantity of items, number of pallets, or weight of the shipment.

92.   Consolidation fees for high-value product are often based on a dollar value per unit, as opposed to a percentage of the shipment's total value.

93.   The return rate for digital cameras is less than two percent of sales.

94.   No trouble found (NTF) rate for digital cameras is less than two percent as compared to other consumer electronics that can have NTF rates as high as forty-five percent.

95.   Retailers that sell high-end women's apparel have the highest return rate of any retail format, ranging from twenty-five to as much as forty-five percent of sales.

96.   It is against federal law to sell a returned PC as new, if another customer has opened the box and turned it on.

97.   It is NOT against the law to re-sell undergarments as new, even if they may have been worn by a previous customer who returned it.

98.   An advanced exchange program is a program where the customer notifies the seller that their unit does not operate; the seller immediately sends a replacement to the customer; and the customer has thirty to ninety days to return the defective unit or they will be charged for the new unit by the seller.

99.   Gift cards significantly reduce Christmas returns.

100. Most catalogue and Internet retailers that sell apparel will re-package and sell returned items as new items if the garment is not stained, has no odor, and does not look worn.

101. The worst job in the reverse logistics industry is the olfactory engineer. This is the person whose job it is to sniff returned undergarments and other clothing to see if the garments have been worn or if they can be resold as new.

Bibliography

1. "Reverse Logistics: Driving Improved Returns Directly to the Bottom Line" Aberdeen Group, February 2010.
2. Dr. James R. Stock and Dr. Jay P. Mulki. Product Returns Processing: An Examination of Practices of Manufacturers, Wholesalers/Distributors, and Retailers". Journal of Business Logistics, Volume 30, Number 1, 2009.
3. Greve, Curtis. "Why Every Manufacturer Should Focus on Reverse Logistics". http://grevedavis.com/2011/07/20/why-every-manufacturer-should-focus-on-reverse-logistics/ (20 July 2011)
4. Dr. Dale S. Rogers, Dr. Ronald S. Lembke and Zachary S. Rogers. "Creating value through product stewardship and take-back Sustainability Accounting, Management and Policy Journal Volume: 1 Issue 2 2010
5. 2010 Customer Returns in the Retail Industry. The National Retail Federation. 2011
6. "Revisiting Reverse Logistics in the Customer-Centric Service Chain" Aberdeen Group, September 2006.
7. Greve, Curtis. "Customer Return Policies". Greve, Curtis. "Why Every Manufacturer Should Focus on Reverse Logistics". Http://grevedavis.com/2011/07/20/why-every-manufacturer-should-focus-on-reverse-logistics/ (12 February 2011)

8.   Personal interview with Curtis Greve, Principal, Greve-Davis, Pittsburgh, PA, 29 July 2010.

9.   Dr. Dale S. Rogers and Dr. Ronald S. Tibben-Lembke. <u>Going Backwards: Reverse Logistics Trends and Practices</u>. Reverse Logistics Executive Council, © 1998.

10.   Dr. J. Andrew Petersen and Dr. V. Kumar. "Can Product Returns Make You Money?." <u>MIT Sloan Management Review</u>, Spring 2010 Vol. 51 No. 3 pp. 85-89.

11.   Personal interview with Dr. Dale S. Rogers, Professor of Supply Chain Management and Marketing Science at Rutgers University Pittsburgh, PA, 15 May 2010.

12.   Personal interview with Jerry Davis, Principal, Greve-Davis, Savannah, GA, 29 July 2010.

13.   <u>2009 Customer Returns in the Retail Industry</u>. The National Retail Federation. 2010

14.   Personal interview with Jerry Davis and Curtis Greve, Principals, Greve-Davis, Savannah, GA, 29 July 2010.

15.   Aftermarket News staff. "The Pulse: Reasons for Returns". http://www.counterman.com/Article/78477/the_pulse_reasons_for_returns.aspx (20 August 2010)

16.   Podcast with Curtis Greve and Dr. Dale S. Rogers "Sustainable Supply Chain Management". http://grevedavis.com/blog/podcasts/

17.   Terra Choice Environmental Marketing Inc. "<u>The Six Sins of Greenwashing</u>" November 2007

18.   Personal comment posted on a survey by Dr. Mark Ferguson, Adjunct Associate Professor at Georgia Tech University, March 2010.

19.   Allen L. White, Ph.D, Mark Stoughton, and Linda Feng. "<u>Servicizing: The Quiet Transition to Extended Product Responsibility</u>". Submitted to the U.S. environmental Protection Agency Office of Solid Waste May 1999

Made in the USA
Charleston, SC
11 March 2012